NORMAN ROCKWELL'S PEOPLE

Susan E. Meyer

NORMAN ROCKWELL'S PEOPLE

Harrison House / Harry N. Abrams, Inc.

New York

FOR MARSHA

Editor: Edith M. Pavese
Designer: Patrick Cunningham
Rights and Reproductions: Barbara Lyons

Library of Congress Cataloging-in-Publication Data
Meyer, Susan E.
  Norman Rockwell's people.
  Reprint. Originally published: New York:
H. N. Abrams, 1981.
  Includes index.
  1. Rockwell, Norman, 1894–1978.   2. Painters—
United States—Biography.   I. Title.
[ND237.R68M49   1987]   759.13   [B]   86–19494
ISBN 0–517–62354–4

This 1987 edition published by Harrison House/Harry N. Abrams, Inc.,
distributed by Crown Publishers, Inc., 225 Park Avenue South, New York,
New York 10003

h g f e d c b a

Printed and bound in Hong Kong

Contents

Acknowledgments

It would have been impossible to venture into Rockwell's past without the guidance of Rockwell's people. "Another Rockwell book?" I heard many times from those who were weary of such interviews. It was their love for Norman Rockwell that rallied them for this project, because they knew I was looking at the subject afresh with the generous assistance of the Rockwell family itself. With almost no exception, I was received with an overwhelming warmth and enthusiasm as I returned to Rockwell's haunts and friends with tape recorder in hand. The following people were interviewed for this book, and to them all I owe my sincerest thanks:

MAXINE ATHERTON
MARY ATHERTON VARCHEVER
JOHN BENEDICT
HANK BERGMANS
HENRY BERGMANS
MARIE BRIGGS
LESTER BRUSH
MRS. LAWRENCE BRUSH
DR. DONALD CAMPBELL
DORIS CROFUT WRIGHT
ROY CROFUT
JANET CROSS KEOUGH
YVONNE CROSS DORR
FRANK DOLSON
ARDIS EDGERTON CLARK

BUDDY EDGERTON
CLARA EDGERTON
EDITH EDGERTON ZINDEL
JOY EDGERTON FREISATZ
CARL HESS
MRS. ROSE HOYT
GEORGE HUGHES
JACKIE JAMES WALKER
WALTER KELLY
LOUIE LAMONE
FRANKLIN LISCHKE
ED LOCKE
DAVID LOVELESS
MOE AND JOAN MAHONEY
ANN MARSH

PATRICK O'NEIL
JARVIS ROCKWELL
MOLLY ROCKWELL
PETER ROCKWELL
RICHARD ROCKWELL
TOM ROCKWELL
LEE SCHAEFFER GOODFELLOW
MEAD SCHAEFFER
MARY AND CHRIS SCHAFER
WALTER SCOTT
DON SPAULDING
LUCILLE TOWNE HULTON
MARY WHALEN LEONARD

Each of those interviewed helped me identify Rockwell's models from the paintings, a process that became a marvelous detective game. Because I discovered that this who's who is fascinating to Rockwell admirers, I include the names of all the models made known to me (about 140 of them!), apologizing in advance for those who may still remain anonymous and for some inadvertent misidentifications. The detective hunt will certainly continue after this book is published.

One individual in this list deserves a special note of thanks for her extra care and consideration in making my job not only easier but downright enjoyable. From the first day I met Clara Edgerton at a family gathering in Arlington, I knew we would be friends. She squired me everywhere, into the homes of her neighbors and through the hills overlooking the Batten Kill River. If ever there was such a thing as southern hospitality in Vermont, Clara extended it to me.

Having dealt with the families of important people before, I was prepared for the tension that often arises when delicate family issues run the risk of exposure. Not so with the Rockwell family. With the Rockwells, matters of delicacy are matters for laughter, introspection, examination, perhaps, but *not* for secrecy. "Ask me any questions you have about my father. I'll be as interested in exploring the answers as you are," assured Jarvis Rockwell. For their candor, generosity, and humor I am most thankful to Tom, Peter, Jarvis, and Molly Rockwell. The family's close reading of my text was extremely helpful in correcting several inaccuracies that have been perpetuated through the years, and I am particularly grateful to Tom Rockwell for giving me the exclusive right to publish several of his mother's letters about her husband. Written in 1932, and never before published, these letters provide an extraordinary insight into Mary and Norman Rockwell's relationship and describe vividly the artist's struggle with his work.

If the family proved supportive, the custodians of the Norman Rockwell estate were equally helpful to me in writing this book. David Wood, the Director of the Old Corner House in Stockbridge, and Laurie Norton, the registrar, could not have been more cooperative in providing me with photographs taken directly from Norman Rockwell's personal photographic file and for their guidance through the morass of information at my disposal. My gift to the Old Corner House of the tapes from my interviews with Rockwell's people will hardly be thanks enough for their help.

Others along the way have provided invaluable help as well. Linda Davidson had an extremely rich interview with Peter Rockwell in Rome, providing much material for the book, for which I am grateful. Judy and Alan Goffman and Martin Diamond were most generous in lending me Rockwell transparencies so that so many of the *original* paintings could be reproduced for the first time.

At the publishing company of Harry N. Abrams I have many friends who guided this book through some stormy seas. In particular, I give my special thanks to Lena Tabori, who recognized I was ready to write another book after a two-year hiatus and rushed to encourage me at a time when I was afflicted with many self-doubts about returning to the typewriter. Edith Pavese, Barbara Lyons, and Patrick Cunningham were an unbeatable team in ushering the book from concept to design. If this book is successful, it's because all these professionals had confidence in me.

Finally, my family, to whom I always owe so much. My mother, now most skilled at tolerating the changeable temperaments of the writers in her family, gave me great encouragement. And to my extended family, Rosemary and Wayne Blake, my debt of gratitude is everlasting. Without their support—in more ways than one—this book might never have come to pass. Norman Rockwell forms a personal bond between us, a bond that made it possible for me to undertake entirely new directions in my work.

And to Marsha Melnick, my best friend and business partner, I give my thanks for her unfaltering trust through so many firsts.

DIRECTORY OF ROCKWELL'S PEOPLE

JOHN ATHERTON 93

MARY ATHERTON 167

BYRNE BAUER 208

ART BECKTOFT 136

JOHN BENEDICT 168

ROBERT BENEDICT, SR. 129

ROBERT BENEDICT, JR. 168

FLOYD BENTLEY 157

HANK BERGMANS 203

BOZO 144

JASON BRAMAN 197

BARBARA BROOKS 208

BOB BROOKS 208

BILLIE BROWN 115

142

HARRY BROWN 129

ANN BRUSH 145

JOHN BRUSH 145

LARRY BRUSH 145

LESTER BRUSH 58

131

148

MARJORY BRUSH 145

ROBERT OTIS BUCK

109
122

122

122

122

123

123

123

125

127

BETSY CAMPBELL 201

DR. DONALD CAMPBELL 202

DAVE CAMPION 46

47

TOM CAREY 207

EDDIE CARSON 35

DICK CLEMENS 205

CORDELIA COMAR 58

MR. COMAR 134

DWIGHT COWAN 148

OSCEOLLA CRANDALL 208

CHARLES CROFUT 142

MRS. CHARLES CROFUT 141

DORIS CROFUT 58

RENA CROFUT 58

167

ROY CROFUT 109

143

GLADYS CROSS 109

JANET CROSS 143

JOHN CROSS, JR. 115

JOHN CROSS, SR. 115

YVONNE CROSS 109

115

CLARENCE DECKER 79

85

138

FRANK DOLSON 211

211

ARDIS EDGERTON 115

BUDDY EDGERTON

95   104   111   112   113   114

CLARA EDGERTON

108   108   109

JIM EDGERTON

109
122

JIMMY
EDGERTON   POP FREDERICKS

114   47   48   48   48

GENT   FREEMAN GROUT   FRANK HALL

142   177   177   58

KEN HALL   AMELIA
HARRINGTON   MRS. JESSIE
HARRINGTON   JESSIE
HARRINGTON   CARL HESS   HENRY HESS

208   130   58   58   104   129   129   139

FRED HILDEBRANDT   HOISINGTON
CHILDREN   IRENE HOYT   ROSE HOYT   MARY IMMEN

54   54   54   55   131   115   129   130   235   167

OLIVER
KEMPTON   LOUIE LAMONE   ALBERT LA BOMBARD   ELIZABETH
LA BOMBARD   MRS. EDGAR
LAWRENCE   FLORENCE
LINDSEY   CHARLES
LINDSEY

208   199   199   208   115   134   115   132   131   131

FRANKLIN LISCHKE

42   42   43   44   44   44   44   45   45   45

ED LOCKE   DAVID LOVELESS   JIM McCABE   HARVEY McKEE   JENNY McKEE

202   205   199   208   235   138   139   58   115   141

JOAN AND MOE MAHONEY 197

JOHN L. MALONE 46

ANN MARSH 167

CHUCK MARSH 150 151 167

DON MARSH 151 167

JIM MARTIN 129 130 131 132

ANNE MORGAN 201

GRANDMA MOSES 167

NIP NOYES 139 139

168

BILL OBANHEIM 208

SHARON O'NEIL 167 167

BILLY PAINE 34

GENE PELHAM 84 103 108 109 122

171

DUANE PETERS 134 168

CYNTHIA ROCKWELL 181

GAIL ROCKWELL 211 231

GEOFFREY ROCKWELL 235

JARVIS ROCKWELL 165 167 168 171 173

MARY ROCKWELL 58 131 163 167 235

MOLLY ROCKWELL 190 232

MRS. NANCY ROCKWELL 131

PETER ROCKWELL 167 168 176 177 177 112 177 179 181

TOM ROCKWELL 112 115 164 167 174 174 175

DR. GEORGE RUSSELL 144

ELIZABETH
SCHAEFFER

LEE SCHAEFFER

MEAD SCHAEFFER

85 86 86 87 87 87
122 94 167 79 167

PATTY SCHAEFFER CHRIS SCHAFER CHRISTINE SCHAFER

86 94 167 118 119 119 235 94 119

JOHN SCHAFER MARY SCHAFER HARRY SEAL FRANK
SECOY

BILL SHARKEY

119 121 118 119 49 49 49 130 171

WALT SMITH SPOT CLARA
SQUIRES

SQUIRES
CHILDREN

HERB SQUIRES WALT SQUIRES ED SULLIVAN BILL
SUNDERMEYER

134 115 130 132 168 88 130 139 208 47

JAMES K. VAN BRUNT

50 50 50 51 51 51 52 53 53 53

MRS. RALPH
WALKER

MARY WHALEN MRS. WHEATON MR. WHEATON ORIN WILCOX BOB WILLIAMS JAMES WILSON

171 151 153 155 131 131 87 208 46

DON WINSLOW MRS. GEORGE
ZIMMER

GEORGE ZIMMER

103 171 58 58 134

Artist Before a Blank Canvas. Saturday Evening Post cover, October 8, 1938.

Preface

Unlike most of his admirers, I was not introduced to Norman Rockwell through the pages of the *Saturday Evening Post*. I would have to say that my family considered itself a bit too high brow to fancy the prose and pictures of the weekly magazine as a regular diet, so I never recall seeing a copy of the *Post* when I was a child. By the time I was developing my own patterns of reading, the magazine—sinking badly—had already left me behind.

It was not until I landed an editorial job at Watson-Guptill Publications in 1963, shortly after graduating from college, that I discovered Norman Rockwell. Assigned to study all the books written by the company's founders, I was directed to *Norman Rockwell Illustrator* by Arthur L. Guptill. Released in 1946—and long out of print—this was at that point the only volume ever published on the illustrator. (The book was reissued twenty-five years later by the same publisher.) Through reading this publication I made several discoveries about art and writing, discoveries that dramatically altered the direction of my career. Fresh from my art history courses at the university, I had regarded the field of art and art criticism as somehow sacrosanct: art discussion required a reverential tone and a special vocabulary, and true artists were never commercial. Arthur Guptill's book challenged all that. The author's tone was personal, downright *friendly*, and the illustrator's work fascinated me. How could I reconcile these contradictions? My comfortable prejudices began to shatter. Was art *meant* to be accessible to a popular audience? Was art writing *meant* to be understood by everyone? After all, there must be *some* standards to uphold!

I struggled with this thought for some time and concluded that I had learned more about the creative process by reading Guptill's book than I had by reading all those lofty tomes and painstaking criticism required by my courses in college. There was nothing painful here: Norman Rockwell was a joy.

As an artist himself, Arthur Guptill was particularly concerned with process— how an artist converts that vague sense of an idea into something concrete. In his writing Guptill conveyed both the drama and tedium involved in creative execution, not embarrassed to display his own child-like excitement for the subject. Through his writing the reader is *with* the artist, not *above* him, an empathy I found refreshing. In subsequent years my enthusiasm for Guptill inspired me to adapt several of his art instruction books—written in the 1920s for the most part—to a contemporary audience, and my own writing became more approachable as I gained confidence in the notion that *art* is approachable.

If Guptill introduced me to a way of writing about artists, Norman Rockwell introduced me to the world of illustration, one I had never known before. This was no second-rate hack selling his soul for commerce. He was proud of his calling, considered himself part of an important tradition. Here was a story-teller in a contemporary context performing some of the same commercial functions the Old Masters had performed for their patrons. The humor was gentle, without rancor, and the scenes were familiar to me. Beyond the content, however, was the extraordinary skill he demonstrated. His sense of composition and color was superb, his draftsmanship impeccable. He was, as Peter Rockwell has called him, "a thinking painter." And he was a revelation to me.

My only regret is not having met Rockwell when I was first so inspired by his work. By the time I became acquainted with him in 1975, he was already in decline. Then Editor of *American Artist* magazine, I had commissioned the elderly illustrator to paint a cover for our bicentennial issue. During the months he worked on the painting, I visited with him several times and offered my suggestions when he asked for them. I felt deeply touched by the sadness that flickered through his frail blue eyes, and I was aware that he seemed embarrassed by the indignity of being held captive by age. It was hard not to reach out and embrace him, to protect him from what must have been humiliating exposure for the distinguished artist. I must have known then that his painting for *American Artist* would be his last magazine cover.

To prepare for his book in 1945, Arthur Guptill ventured to Arlington, Vermont, where Norman Rockwell was then living. During Guptill's stay he met many of the people mentioned in this book. It did not escape me that I was making the same trip thirty-five years later. Rockwell had moved from Arlington years before, and many of his friends were gone, but I found much of the past still vibrant in Arlington. My time there made clear to me that Rockwell's emotional bond between the people in his life and the people in his pictures was strongest in Arlington, which explains why so much of this book is devoted to his friends, neighbors, and paintings from that location.

The information obtained for the text of this book was gathered directly from Rockwell's people and from his own photographic files in his Stockbridge studio. The only published material used for reference was what Rockwell himself had written. Occasionally I refer to his book adapted from his course at the Famous Artists Schools, called *Rockwell on Rockwell* (Watson-Guptill, 1979), and throughout this book I have quoted from

Rockwell's superb autobiography, My *Adventures as an Illustrator* (Double-day, 1960). The latter is the single most valuable source of information on Norman Rockwell, documenting not only the events in his life, but the illustrator's charming character as well. One word of caution: Rockwell's own writing does not, in itself, guarantee the accuracy of the information. Rockwell's version of the past is not always entirely reliable. "My father believed that the truth was interesting only so long as it didn't disturb a good story," observed Peter Rockwell.

On the other hand, *Norman Rockwell's People* was not designed to be a systematically organized documentary. Although the material here derives from original sources, the book is not a biography. On the contrary, these recollections are what might be termed "sketches from life," fragments drawn from memories and assembled to form a composite portrait of the illustrator. There are, of course, certain consequences that result from this unorthodox approach. The form and content of the information were necessarily determined by the number and nature of the people inter-viewed. Because of this fact, a few observations are in order here.

In this book, I have made every effort to record accurately what Rock-well's friends remembered and how they narrated these remembrances, and in so doing I surrendered to the idiosyncrasies inherent in the way memory tends to function. I asked Rockwell's friends and relatives to reach back many years, to recall impressions and events that may have occurred as long as forty years earlier. (One even reached back sixty years!) Reviving the past generally means fastening onto two extreme methods of recall: through explicit details or through broad impressions; either too much detail or too little. Portrayal of the past tends to be subjective, demonstrating as much about the people themselves as it does about the subject at hand. Contra-dictory impressions can be reconciled only by considering their source. A single characteristic—was Rockwell shy, for example—would be inter-preted one way by a son, another way by a colleague from the city, and another way by a farmer living next door in Vermont. In fact, the compos-ite portrait must allow for the very complexities of Rockwell's temperament that would reveal to some his urbane, party-loving nature, and to others his retiring and somewhat bashful character. I have considered all these im-pressions equally valid, maintaining that human nature cannot be so neatly compartmentalized, regardless of the journalistic temptation to select and exaggerate for the sake of a good story.

Consequently, I have not attempted to reconcile what may appear to be contradictory observations. Only where memory was clearly inaccurate in recalling precise facts—dates, names, or similar data—have I altered the information presented by Rockwell or by his people. I must emphasize, however, that these lapses in interpretation affect only the nuances of the total picture. The consistencies of general impression far outweigh the discrepancies in detail.

The number of people interviewed was dictated by those who still survive, and by their particular rapport with the illustrator. Several individuals intimately connected to Rockwell have passed away: his professional models, two of his three wives, and some of his closest friends, such as Jim Edgerton, Jack Atherton, Harry Dwight, to name a few. (Mead Schaeffer died only four weeks after I had talked with him.) Clearly, I was racing against time to reach the older friends who still remain, having already lost the opportunity of meeting some of the most significant.

Judging from all the interviews held for this book, I concluded that Norman Rockwell had no enemies in his lifetime. Being loved was essential for him—whether this was achieved through the covers of America's most beloved magazine, or through a casual "hello" called out to a neighbor on a street corner. "He made you feel important" was a theme consistently restated by those who knew him. His warmth was the lifeblood of his work and of his connection to everyone he encountered throughout his life.

As can be expected, his good nature won him many friends, but also attracted opportunists. He wrote checks freely, gave away paintings casually, and frequently opened his studio to his admirers. Naturally, such generosity invited its share of avarice. "None of Norman's closest friends ever owned an original Rockwell," one friend observed. "You got a painting only by asking for one, because Norman was too embarrassed to offer—thinking it a pretentious gift—and his good friends were too embarrassed to ask."

The avarice that continues to flourish indirectly affected this book. Two gentlemen who were regular recipients of Rockwell's generosity refused an interview when they heard I was not buying information. (My pride and principles prevented me from accepting their terms. Although the presence of these individuals is sorely missed from these pages, I feel certain that history will exonerate me from such omission.) In fairness, such opportunism is obviously a factor of the astonishing commercial rewards derived from Rockwell's art. Signed reproductions have escalated in price since his passing. Porcelain figurines whose three-dimensionality violate his art continue to sell for inflated prices. The value of Rockwell's originals matches those of the nineteenth-century masters. Tourism to Rockwell's hometown is profitable to the commercial community. Such events in the marketplace can surely exaggerate even the most modest character flaws in an individual. It is ironic, indeed, that those who have gained from these exorbitant profits are often those who commend Rockwell for his "humility."

Fortunately, the opportunists in his life represented a minority of his friends. In nearly every instance friends and acquaintances expressed a strong sense of privilege for having known him at all. These are the individuals selected for interview, and their recollections constitute the major content of this volume. Even years later, the memory of the artist as a modest and thoughtful man emerges clearly, and all those I interviewed were eager to return the kindness he had extended to them. Their eagerness to work with me derives from their enduring loyalty to Rockwell's gentle nature. Dr. Campbell in Stockbridge expressed it eloquently: "I would happily put my small contribution toward anything that redounds to his memory." Rockwell's fans may have tramped the gardens around his home, peered through the windows of his studio, pulled at his sleeve for an autograph, but Rockwell's friends continue to respect the privacy of their good friend. Their discretion on matters of delicacy described more about their affection for the family than any of the most explicit anecdotes might have revealed.

Although they are loyal, Rockwell's people are not reverential. They talked expansively about their good friend, without enshrining him in piety. I sensed that they felt fortunate in knowing him because he was a fine human being first and foremost, not because he was a genius in their midst. His family, friends, and neighbors regarded him as one of them, not superior to them, a true credit to his affable and modest nature.

It is extraordinary that one illustrator has managed to maintain such phenomenal preeminence for so many years. He is as beloved posthumously as he was when he was the *Post*'s child wonder in 1916. There were other illustrators who achieved considerable fame in their lifetime, but none who sustained the consistent enthusiasm of the public for so many decades. There are illustrators who have become obscure, even though their images may still be familiar. Uncle Sam's "I Want You" poster, for example, is far better known than its originator, James Montgomery Flagg. The Arrow Collar Man is generally not associated with its creator, J.C. Leyendecker. Although the *Post* certainly provided the visibility that made Rockwell familiar to millions, he never painted more than eleven covers in any one year for the weekly, and the less familiar J.C. Leyendecker illustrated nearly as many during *his* lifetime.

Norman Rockwell, more than any of his colleagues, was tapping themes that have endured. His vision of humanity transcended current fashion and events by reaching into the deeper recesses of our dreams and memories. It was not the War he depicted, for example, but the soldier's homecoming; it was not the Depression he illustrated, but the cherished moments between father and son. The yearnings for tenderness, for laughter, for peace have not changed with the fashions, and his pictures continue to have meaning.

Rockwell's paintings were an extension of the man. He believed in what he painted. His humanity was genuine, and what the public loved in his paintings his friends loved in him. In the end, it was his temperament—as much as his artistic gift—that made him America's favorite illustrator.

Susan E. Meyer
New York City, 1981

The Connoisseur. Original oil painting for a *Saturday Evening Post* cover, January 13, 1962. Private collection.

Introduction

Norman Rockwell never experienced real hardship in getting started, unlike most illustrators. His work was published regularly by the time he was eighteen years old, and he sold his first cover to the *Post* when he was only twenty-two. But Rockwell was not alone in his calling. He began his career in an environment that was receptive to his talents. A variety of forces at the turn of the century made it possible for Rockwell, and others like him, to rise to preeminence.

The Ennobling Profession

"To us illustration was an ennobling profession," Rockwell maintained. "That's part of the reason I went into illustration. It was a profession with a great tradition, a profession I could be proud of."

This profession Rockwell refers to may have had a great tradition, but it was not a very long one. American illustration had come into its own only during the Civil War, and Rockwell entered the limelight just when it had reached its heyday. Illustration had become the most significant way for business to reach a wide, popular audience. Only through printed images could books, magazines, and merchandise be sold effectively. Because illustration influenced so much commerce, these artists were in great demand by publishers and manufacturers; the potential for a talented and ambitious illustrator was enormous. As a result, book and magazine illustrators were the celebrities and heroes of their day. The tremendous activity in advertising and in book and periodical publishing—adult and children's books, family magazines, youth magazines, humor magazines—produced a diverse group of clients and a selection of specialized illustrators to serve them.

There were, in fact, more opportunities than there were artists. Every editor and publisher competed fiercely for the limited supply of talent available to them. With their extravagant promotion and their vast circulations, magazines constituted the most spectacular—if not the most enduring—showcase for creative talent. Radio, motion pictures, and television would eclipse the printed word and picture as the greatest source of public entertainment, but until their arrival the magazine captured the exclusive attention of millions of Americans and, like the newer arrivals, represented in their day a particular form of show business.

Norman Rockwell, therefore, was not alone in his status as a celebrity. He was part of a respected group of professionals who had captured the public's imagination with visual images. "We were exalted in those days," recalled Mead Schaeffer shortly before he passed away in 1980. "Do you know what it's like to be venerated just for doing what you love to do?"

Out of all this activity developed illustrators of a wide variety of artistic persuasions. There was the group from the Brandywine River Valley near Wilmington, Delaware, for example, whose members derived inspiration from their mentor, Howard Pyle. This was an inspired crew of painters, including N.C. Wyeth and Frank Schoonover, who knew just how to inject drama and reality into classic, heroic tales of adventure, stories in which chivalry and daring were virtues of the highest order. Then there were the decorative illustrators—Will Bradley and Maxfield Parrish, for example—whose talents were ideal for posters and magazine covers where pleasing line, space, and flat colors would tantalize the eye of the casual passer-by. There were the humorists—such as James Montgomery Flagg and John Held—and the chic New York illustrators—such as Charles Dana Gibson and Harrison Fisher—who portrayed fashionable society in sophisticated situations. Cartoons and classics; children's stories; sports and fashion; the Wild West: all described through alluring images and delivered as a regular diet to the American public.

Rockwell felt an artistic kinship to all these illustrators—with particular admiration for Howard Pyle—and he was like them in many ways. Almost without exception, these popular heroes shared a natural affinity for the American ideals of the Victorian and Edwardian eras, and they expressed these views in their work and in their personal philosophies. Their attitudes provided an important function in a nation creating an identity out of a cauldron of mixed ethnic ingredients. Through pictures of urban and rural life, these popular illustrators provided the public with its first image of American ideals. All readers could confirm their American identity through these artists, and the thousands of immigrants pouring into the country each day would find in the pages of American magazines prototypes after which they could pattern themselves. The Gibson Girl and the Arrow Collar Man became symbols of the ideal American, and Rockwell's pictures described universal human experiences placed within a particularly American context.

For their skills, the illustrators were amply rewarded and lived well from the extravagant sums they received. As early as 1903, for example, Charles Dana Gibson was awarded a contract from *Collier's* for one hundred pen-and-ink drawings at the fee of $100 each. The publications treated their artists with respect. The established illustrators were regarded as authorities on the tastes of their public and most publications gave them total freedom. (It was not until the arrival of the so-called "art director" that the control shifted

The Gibson Girl by Charles Dana Gibson.

from artist to publisher, a transition most illustrators found abhorrent.) These attractions—the freedom to be creative and the commensurate rewards—made illustration a most attractive field to pursue.

But it took more than ambition and talent to establish an illustrator. Temperament was also a factor. The ingredients necessary in this area were common to all those who succeeded, and Norman Rockwell especially shared these required traits.

First, illustration required discipline. After all, vast sums of money were invested in fixed publishing dates and the illustrator was obliged to withstand the pressures and meet deadlines reliably—without sacrificing the quality of his work in the process. This meant sustained application; no time for excessive indulgence in personal pains and pleasures that might prove distracting. Stability was crucial. Such application required a genuine passion for work. Without exception, all the illustrators of their day shared this passion. Work was their joy, their pain, their sustenance. They could not survive without it. Although a very different illustrator from Rockwell, N.C. Wyeth was convinced of the need for discipline, and put it this way: "There's only one kind of work that counts, and that is constant, sustained effort. Drive, drive, drive in the one direction—painting. Without a break. It is the only way any man ever accomplished anything worthwhile."

While discipline and hard work required hours alone in the studio, the illustrator could not succeed by working exclusively in isolation. Collaboration with others was constantly required. To work with editors, models, writers, he had to be flexible, efficient, good natured. A sense of humor helped, too. He had to learn how to surrender his pride if an editor rejected an idea or suggested changes; he had to conform to restrictions of size, color, and subject that might be placed on him by a publication. Rockwell was not unaware of this need for humility when he wrote in his autobiography,

> A fine arts painter has to satisfy only himself. No outside restrictions are imposed on his work. The situation is very different in commercial art. The illustrator must satisfy his client as well as himself. He must express a specific idea so that a large number of people will understand it; and there must be no mistake as to what he is trying to convey. Then there are the deadlines, taboos as to subject matter; . . . the proportions of the picture must conform to the proportions of the magazine. Most fine arts painters feel that these restrictions constitute pure slavery.

It was impossible for an illustrator to remain distant from the practicalities his profession demanded. It was equally undesirable for him to remain distant from his public. After all, his work was popular only as long as he continued to appeal to the appetites of the day. Unless he was prepared to face the consequences of falling behind the times, he simply had to keep up

to date. "To stay in touch with the trend," Rockwell said, "I keep my ear so close to the ground it's full of dirt." The very best illustrators—Norman Rockwell and N.C. Wyeth among them—were able to stay in touch with contemporary tastes, without disrupting the features that made them unique as artists. But the tension was always there; the uncertainty that fickle Time would shove the illustrator aside. Knowing the penalty for careless repetition, these illustrators were ever vigilant.

These generalizations about illustrators may help explain why they were so self-sufficient as a group, and why there was a strong sense of camaraderie among them. For the most part, they enjoyed each other's company. They tended to be witty, urbane, and well informed. The illustrators derived enormous pleasure from their success—the material comforts as well as the psychic rewards from having received public recognition for their private

ABOVE
Winter by N. C. Wyeth. Original oil painting for "The Moods" by George T. Marsh for *Scribner's Magazine*, December, 1909.

RIGHT
A Swiss Admiral by Maxfield Parrish. Original oil painting, 1910. Private collection.

FAR RIGHT
Side by Side—Britannia! by James Montgomery Flagg. World War I poster, 1918. Collection Susan E. Meyer.

efforts. There was enough prosperity, both actual and spiritual, that they tended to be non-competitive with each other, free of jealous yearnings. The illustrators respected each other's work and shared the tensions that deadlines always pressed upon them. They asked and took advice freely, accustomed to being objective about the success or failure of a current project. They knew how to have a good time. Because of their gift for fantasy they enjoyed games and costume parties; they loved good food, literature, and—always—good art. They had reason to be proud and they knew it.

The Next Picture

"I think my work is improving. I start each picture with the same high hopes, and if I never seem able to fulfill them I still try my darnedest."

Each morning Norman Rockwell entered his studio and set into motion a process that continued to challenge him for over sixty years. Each painting renewed him. He was consumed by the process. Like an athlete in training, he exercised daily and was always preparing for the next feat before him. From the painful formation of an idea, the artist moved quite methodically and deliberately to the completion of the canvas, a process that required

concentration and patience, for the painting rarely developed without at least a troubled moment or two. There was, of course, the jubilance generally experienced at the earliest stage of painting, and there were the familiar frustrations that could seem unendurable. A painting could take anywhere from three days to three months to meet his standards; the average painting took about three weeks. And many were discarded along the way. This was all part of the process that drove him year after year, until he could paint no more.

To set the process in motion, Rockwell tended to follow a rather straightforward course. First was the idea. For an advertisement or calendar, the range of ideas was necessarily more restricted because of the nature of the assignments, but with the *Post* Rockwell was given full rein. He would search for an idea "which makes the reader want to sigh and smile at the same time." But the process wasn't easy and he had to work himself up to it.

I know of no painless process for giving birth to a picture idea. When I must produce one, I retire to a quiet room with a supply of cheap paper and sharp pencils. My brain is going to take a beating—and knows it. First I invariably draw a lamp post. I have found that I must start somewhere and if I did not start with the lamp post or something else, I would spend the whole day looking at the blank paper. So I start with hope and prayer—and a lamp post. Next, I draw a drunken sailor clinging to my lamp post. Now I have an object and a person. Then I give my brain a little exercise. Through association of ideas I am reminded that sailors must do their own mending, so I put that down. That reminds me of a mother sewing up Junior's trousers with Junior in them, and I draw that. At last I am on my way, but where I will end I never know. I keep hoping and praying for a knockout idea. And I keep on making sketches. Usually the first session gets me nowhere. Most authors, composers, playwrights, and other creative people seem to have the same experience. Somehow you must condition

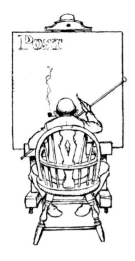

Norman Rockwell From the Cradle to the Grave. Reproduced from Norman Rockwell, Illustrator by Arthur L. Guptill. Courtesy Watson-Guptill Publications.

your brain to think creatively. So I generally end this first session of two hours or more completely discouraged. I feel that I never will develop another idea as long as I live.

These words were composed for aspiring students at his course at the Famous Artists Schools, encouraging them to try harder. In his autobiography, Rockwell lamented on the same subject, "I never saw an idea happen or received one, whoosh, from heaven while I was ever washing my brushes or shaving or backing the car out of the garage. I had to beat them out of my head or at least maul my brain until something came out of it. It always seemed to me that it was like getting blood from a stone, except of course that eventually something always came."

Once his ideas were put in some recognizable form, he would show his sketch to friends and family. "If people seem uninterested or only mildly interested, I abandon the idea and search for another," he remarked. "Only when people become enthusiastic do I become enthusiastic too, and then I am anxious to get to painting."

The hunt would then begin for the right model, props, and costumes. Here he would go to any length for authenticity. Peter Rockwell remembered his father telling him about the time he exchanged clothing with a derelict in Hannibal, Missouri, because he found the shabby clothes ideal for illustrating *Tom Sawyer*. Over the years, Rockwell managed to acquire a considerable assortment of authentic costumes, a delight for the kids at Halloween, although much of his collection was destroyed when his studio burned down in 1943.

After gathering models and props for the picture, he would set up the model, in costume, and obtain the desired posture or expression. In the earlier years he worked directly from life, later years from photographs, but the session was similar. A foot might be propped by books to hold an awkward pose, a head silhouetted against a white backdrop, and details assembled to form the total composition that would tell the story most directly.

In theory, the progression of stages through a Rockwell painting varied little through the years. Only in practice did the artist deviate from his standard procedures, casting about for a better solution, asking advice, changing his mind, and starting over. Rockwell maintained that he worked in three stages: the first inspired by the notion that he was about to do the greatest of all paintings, followed by the second stage in which he was convinced he had destroyed the painting beyond salvation. (He called this the "oh-my-God-it's-awful" stage.) Finally, if he didn't burn up the canvas as a result of stage two, he moved onto stage three, achieving a more moderate appraisal of the work and bringing it to completion. For the painting, *Just Married*, Rockwell photographed his models in costume on location. (Years before he would have painted them from life in his studio.) He eliminated some reference materials and combined others to create a complete charcoal drawing with the entire composition worked out in detail. An oil sketch, approximately the size of the final reproduction, established color relationships. On the final canvas Rockwell made a pencil outline of the subject, then laid in all the colors, following his charcoal drawing and the color sketch for reference, until he brought the painting to its finish. A painting for the *Post* might require anywhere from one week to several months before he was satisfied. At the opposite extreme, Rockwell had only three days to paint General Eisenhower in 1952, and he somehow managed to do it.

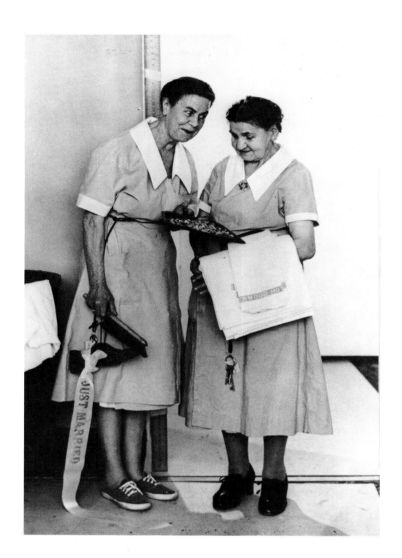

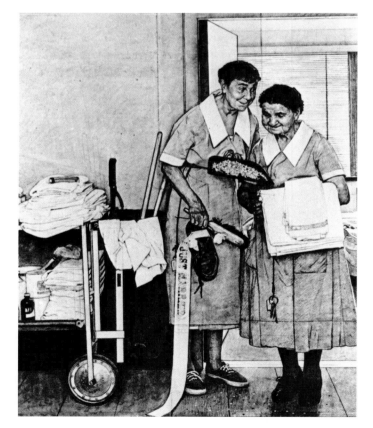

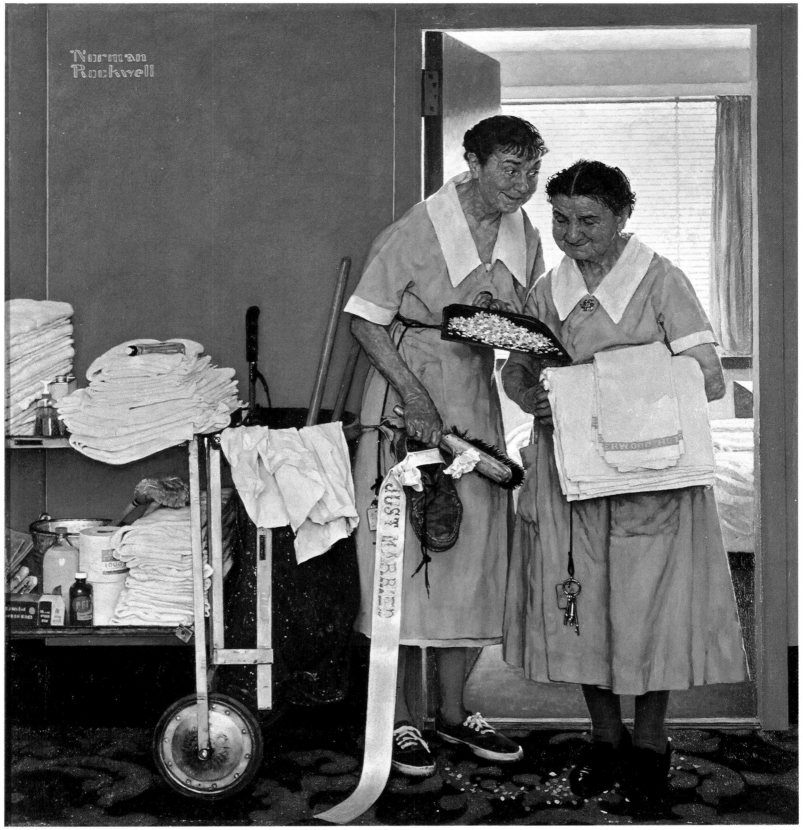

Just Married. Original oil painting for a *Saturday Evening Post* cover, June 29, 1957. Color sketch courtesy Martin Diamond Fine Arts, New York.

Over the years, Rockwell changed his painting procedures, but his general approach remained essentially the same. He would make a detailed drawing in pencil or charcoal—in the same size or slightly smaller than the painting. To accomplish this he resorted to the opaque projector, the balopticon. In his words, "The balopticon is an evil, inartistic, habit-forming, lazy and vicious machine!" Rockwell exclaimed. "It is also a useful, timesaving, practical and helpful one. I use one often—and am thoroughly ashamed of it. I hide it whenever I hear people coming."

Into the projector he placed his original rough sketch, which he had made before he used the models. Then he would set his drawing board on the vertical easel, trying different sizes of enlargement by moving the easel nearer or farther away from the machine until he could determine the appropriate size and proportions.

He drew on architect's detail paper, a dull yellow sheet made in rolls six yards long and forty-two inches wide. Before starting the drawing, he would rub the entire surface with a kneaded eraser to make the surface more receptive to the charcoal. On this surface he began to draw the reflected sketch, lightly and in outline. Then he took the photograph of the most important figure and placed that in the balopticon and enlarged it to the size of the same figure on the enlarged drawing of the sketch. He would then erase the figure in the enlargement of the sketch and in charcoal lightly draw the outline of the figure in the photograph. He did this with each of the details, arriving at a rough idea of how the entire drawing would look. Then he started all over with the main figure and would project it directly on the charcoal outline, drawing in the figure more carefully with a pencil. Along the way, of course, he made many alterations, adapting the image to what his idea was to be.

Changes in the charcoal drawing were relatively easy to accomplish. Rockwell might cut out a section to be changed and substitute a new clean piece with rubber cement. Or he might shift one section of the drawing to another place, adhering the piece to the detail paper with the cement.

This was the phase Rockwell most enjoyed. He completely developed the story and resolved all problems of drawing, composition, and tone—every problem, that is, except color. This stage was to him the very essence of story telling. The simple narrative could be heightened by the wealth of contributing details, none of which was carelessly drawn from imagination. Sometimes it took him as long or even longer to make the charcoal layout than the final painting. He would plan on a week of steady work to complete the drawing.

There were times when he would work out the sketch in great detail *before* he photographed the models. He would then cut apart pieces of individual photographs and lay them down—piece by piece like a jigsaw puzzle—over the drawing, until all pieces were completely assembled in place. Mrs. Hoyt remembered seeing the photograph of her profile added to the others in the sketch after she posed for *Freedom of Worship*.

Rockwell always prepared a small color sketch approximately the size that the image would be reproduced, arranging the color shapes and patterns and judging its overall effectiveness. Normally taking him about a half day to prepare, the color sketch helped him determine the tonal values and the technique he would use for the final painting. (In later years he often painted a color sketch directly over a mat-finish photo print of the charcoal drawing.) Over the color sketch Rockwell placed a clean white mat, the borders of the frame giving him a good environment for judging the color.

The final phase was painting. Rockwell stretched his linen, double-primed canvas and placed it on the easel. By then he had at least one charcoal drawing finished, and the color sketch made. He transferred the image from his full-sized charcoal to the prepared canvas either by tracing or by projecting the image onto his canvas and following the lines. In the first method of transferring, he would lay a sheet of tracing paper over the charcoal and trace the entire subject in pencil. Then he would shift the paper to the canvas, putting a sheet of transfer paper between the tracing and the canvas and following each line on the tracing paper, thereby transferring the image to the canvas. At times, if the tracing was straight-forward, he might hire someone to perform this function for him.

At other times he transferred the image by projecting a photograph of the charcoal drawing directly onto the canvas. The projected forms would then be outlined on the canvas.

After the image was transferred to the canvas, Rockwell sprayed the charcoal with fixative to prevent smudging and then treated the entire surface with a thin wash of oil, toning the surface in what is called an *imprimatura*. After the stained surface was dry, he created an underpainting in monochrome, generally in Mars violet, "to get a feeling of warm humanity." He sealed this underpainting with a light, even coat of shellac, which enabled him if necessary to rub out what he later painted without losing the underpainting below.

Then Rockwell would lay in the colors, an unnerving process for him because of the persistent thoughts racing through his mind as he worked. His greatest fear was that he would kill the painting at this stage by tightening up and destroying the spontaneity of the initial drawing. He went to any extent to prevent this from occurring. "Sometimes, just as an experiment, I paint with a brick or half shingle. You can't be clever or slick with a brick or shingle. You have to paint loosely. And then I've tried painting with my left hand or half asleep or drunk. Anything, so I won't tighten up, anything to break my habit of overworking a head."

This was the process—often laborious and tedious; often exhilarating; always compelling. An average painting might take three weeks—with a minimum of a half day for getting models; three days on the first charcoal; half day on the color sketch; half day stretching canvas; one day on the underpainting; five days on the final painting. Small wonder that Rockwell worked day in and day out to keep up with his deadlines. He was not a fast worker, but he was constant, diligent, and driven.

Rockwell's Early Years

Rockwell's people enter our story in New Rochelle. But where was Norman Rockwell until that time? Let's go back to 1894 when Rockwell was born on 103rd Street and Amsterdam Avenue in New York City. His mother was an Anglophile and named her second son Norman Percevel after Sir Norman Percevel who reputedly kicked Guy Fawkes down the stairs of the Tower of London after he had tried to blow up the House of Lords. In spite of this respectable connection, young Rockwell was ashamed of the appellation and dropped the Percevel as soon as he left home.

Even in his childhood, Rockwell preferred the country to the city, eagerly awaiting the summer months when he would go off to a farm with his family. This preference for the country life continued into later years and formed the basis for his paintings. He found that people from the country were more approachable, more authentic. "Country people do fit my kind of picture better than city people," he explained. "Their faces are more open, expressive, lacking the cold veneer behind which city people seem to hide."

Rockwell's paintings of ungainly adolescents so frequently depicted in later years must have been inspired by his own awkward youth. His older brother Jarvis was athletic and popular, but Rockwell was quite different. "When I got to be ten or eleven and began to be aware of myself and how I stood with the world, I didn't think too much of myself. I could see I wasn't God's gift to man in general, and the baseball coach in particular. A lump, a long skinny nothing, a bean pole without beans—that was what I was." The drive for a place in the sun was directed exclusively toward drawing. "Because it was all I had, I began to make it my whole life. I drew all the time. Gradually my narrow shoulders, long neck, and pigeon toes became less important to me. My feelings no longer paralyzed me. I drew and drew and drew."

Not particularly close to his father, Rockwell remembered that even as children Potty (as he was called by the family) treated them "as sons who've grown up and been away for a long time." Rockwell didn't have much to say about his mother either. Baba, as she was called, seemed afflicted with a variety of illnesses that required continual ministration. ("My father cared for her constantly and with unflagging devotion.") In spite of her illnesses, she lived to be eighty-five.

The Rockwell brothers went different ways. Jarvis, the fine athletic specimen, was extremely successful in business until the Depression. He moved to Kane, Pennsylvania, to design toys for a manufacturer and

Christmas. Saturday Evening Post cover, December 2, 1922.

More than twenty years separated the painting of these two versions of Santa as toymaker. One was created for a magazine cover, the other for a greeting card. Rockwell's consistent and meticulous approach remained constant through the years, making it virtually impossible to determine which was done earlier and which was done later in the artist's career.

Santa with Elves. © Hallmark Cards, Inc., Kansas City, Missouri.

became quite successful at this profession as well. Jarvis was far more restrained than the younger sibling, conservative and correct where Norman tended to be playful and easy-going. In later years they rarely saw each other.

When Rockwell was nine or ten, the family moved to Mamaroneck, a Westchester suburb of New York City, and lived there for a few years until they moved into a boardinghouse in New York City since his mother's illnesses made it difficult for her to attend to household chores. By this time Rockwell had dropped out of highschool to study art full time, first attending the rather stuffy classes at the National Academy of Design where he found that the emphasis was on developing fine artists. He then transferred to the Art Students League, which was more to his liking. At the League there was no distinction made between those preparing for commercial work and those preparing for fine art. As a result, Rockwell obtained a solid education in all aspects of studio work, including an appreciation for the Old Masters which inspired him throughout his career. From his afternoon classes with George Bridgman, Rockwell developed an ability to depict the human figure, and from his morning classes with Thomas Fogarty, he discovered the world of illustration, and was introduced to his favorites—Howard Pyle and Edwin Austin Abbey—through their reproductions. Rockwell always worked hard at his studies and took whatever odd jobs he could in the evening to help finance his art education. It was Fogarty who obtained Rockwell's first commercial assignments. In one of these Rockwell actually earned $150 for ten or twelve drawings made for a children's book called *Tell Me Why Stories*. He was not yet eighteen years old.

By this time Rockwell's family had gone to live in another boardinghouse—Brown Lodge—in New Rochelle, New York. This town was an attractive suburb to other New York City artists and illustrators, such as Frederic Remington, Coles Phillips, and Charles Dana Gibson; cartoonists Clare Briggs and Clyde Forsythe lived in the town, and even J.C. Leyendecker himself—Rockwell's hero—lived there.

Rockwell was illustrating regularly for children's publications—*St. Nicholas, American Boy, Boy's Life, Youth's Companion*—developing a great technique for depicting boys and girls that would later win him more favorable assignments. He rented Frederic Remington's former sculpture studio with his friend Clyde Forsythe, and set himself to the serious task of becoming a professional. In his mind he had a fixed dream: to paint a cover for the *Saturday Evening Post*. Forsythe urged his friend to apply. Rockwell finally prepared two finished paintings and three sketches for the *Post's* editor, George Horace Lorimer. To the young illustrator's astonishment, Lorimer liked all five; he purchased the two finished paintings for $75 and gave Rockwell the approval to polish up the sketches for three more covers. And so began the career with the *Post* that continued uninterrupted for forty-seven years, in which he painted a total of 322 covers.

The year he sold his first cover to the *Post*—in 1916—he proposed to Irene O'Connor, an attractive schoolteacher who was living in Edgewood Hall, the boardinghouse where the Rockwell family had recently moved. They were married not long before Norman Rockwell enlisted in the Navy. Although he was eager to see action in World War I, the Navy kept him in Charleston, South Carolina, to paint portraits and propaganda pieces, and he continued his covers for the *Post*.

Discharged from the Navy after the war, Rockwell resumed his work for the publications and rented a studio from George Lischke over a barn on Prospect Street in New Rochelle, the studio where he worked until 1926 when he finally bought a house at 24 Lord Kichener Road. There Rockwell had a studio designed and constructed for the enormous sum of $18,000.

During these years, Norman and Irene Rockwell tended to go separate ways—he went to Europe twice without her, and he worked at his illustration assiduously, while she acquired her own circle of friends. They were divorced in 1929. Rockwell dismissed the unfortunate match rather uncomfortably in his autobiography: "We got along well together; never quarreled or made a nuisance of ourselves. We gave parties, belonged to a bridge club. Everybody used to like us together. We just didn't love each other, sort of went our own ways. She didn't take any interest in my work. Well, I guess you see what I mean."

For a year Rockwell rattled around in New York City trying to make the best of bachelorhood until he went to California with his friends Clyde and Cotta Forsythe and met Mary Barstow, a twenty-four-year-old schoolteacher from Alhambra. They married in April, 1930, and returned to the house on Lord Kichener Road in New Rochelle. This is where they lived—and where their three sons were born—until they took up permanent residence in Arlington, Vermont, in 1939.

Throughout these years Rockwell produced an enormous amount of work—his covers for the *Post*, of course, but also the Boy Scout calendars, advertising assignments, illustrations for *Tom Sawyer* and *Huckleberry Finn*, and for the magazines *Life*, *Literary Digest*, *Ladies' Home Journal*, and *American* magazine. By the time he left for Arlington, he was one of America's great illustrators, yet his best work still lay ahead of him. From the mid-1940s to the mid-1950s he reached his prime, an amazing achievement for an illustrator who had already been at the top of his profession for over twenty years.

New Rochelle

ANTICS AND ASPIRATIONS

Boy Pushing Baby Carriage. Original oil painting for a *Saturday Evening Post* cover, May 20, 1916. Old Corner House Collection, Stockbridge, Massachusetts.

Boy on Stilts. Saturday Evening Post cover, October 4, 1919.

Young boys and girls constituted many of the models Rockwell used throughout the years, and particularly in New Rochelle. Eddie Carson, shown above, was among Rockwell's favorites of the period. Rockwell also considered Billy Paine, shown left, among his best child models. Posing as all three boys on this, the first Norman Rockwell cover for the *Post,* Billy Paine appeared on fifteen subsequent *Post* covers as well. He was a real prankster. While Rockwell was painting the boy one morning, Paine spotted a policeman through the window, and screamed for help in order to bring the cop running upstairs to the studio. The practical joker had a good laugh over the policeman's disappointment upon discovering nothing wrong. After Billy died (he fell from a window), Rockwell lamented, "He was a swell kid, a regular rapscallion. I missed him a whole lot."

Norman Rockwell launched his professional life from New Rochelle. It was here that he began his association with the *Saturday Evening Post* and developed his distinctive approach to his subject. During his twenty-five years in New Rochelle, Norman Rockwell painted his vision of American life and introduced many of the themes that would continue to appear, in variation, throughout his mature work.

His earliest illustrations for the youth magazines demonstrated a particular knack for depicting the delicate moments of growing up. While he painted the carefree aspects of youth, he was equally sensitive to the awkward embarrassments in boyhood situations, to the pleasures and pains in young romance, and to the childhood yearnings for success. Because these subjects naturally required models that fit the part, locating children for his paintings was a major occupation for the young illustrator from the moment he arrived in New Rochelle.

In his autobiography Rockwell recalls the difficulties he encountered searching out children for subjects; he would hang out in grade schools at recess, peer over fences into back yards, haunt vacant lots, and stop children on the street. By exercising his most persuasive appeals and by offering 50 cents an hour, he might hope to lure a boy from a Saturday ball game. Capturing the boy was only the beginning: next he had to get him to hold the pose long enough for Rockwell to set it down on canvas. It was impossible to have the children assume and hold an entire pose at one time. Instead, if the child happened to be running (which was often the case), he would prop the model's feet into a running position with bricks or boards, making him as comfortable as possible. Then Rockwell would pose the child's right leg and draw that, then the left leg, the right and left arms, head, and finally he would work on the facial expression. Even so, the models would grow restless, squirm and complain. Finally, Rockwell hit upon a system of distracting them that seemed to work. At the beginning of the session he would stack a pile of nickels on a table alongside his easel. Every rest period he would transfer some nickels to the other side of the table, saying, "Now this is your pile," so that the child could see just how much he was earning by holding still. The nickels made a good shiny pile for the older models; with the younger children he used pennies instead, to make even bigger piles that would grow more visibly before their eyes.

The boys were more trouble than the girls, but the girls cost more money. Aside from the model's fee, Rockwell had to pay a chaperone, the mother, or some other accompanying adult. This remained so until the illustrator had developed a reputation for propriety which made it possible for mothers to permit their daughters to pose for him unaccompanied.

These techniques of attracting models, paying them, and piecing together fragments of the figure for the total composition were later adapted to his use of non-professional models and photographing them.

Rockwell recalled that after he'd been in New Rochelle for four or five months, he had developed a list of available models, names and addresses compiled in a notebook, and no longer was obliged to chase kids around the streets. Once he misplaced his notebook and instructed the child to write his name and address on the wall. The next child did the same, and before long all four walls and ceilings were covered with names and addresses, each signature outdoing the previous one for its display value. At least so the story goes.

During this period Billy Paine was a favorite model for Rockwell, posing for the children's magazines and for fifteen *Post* covers. (He posed for all three boys in Rockwell's first *Post* cover.) After a while the young boy became too conceited about his popularity with Rockwell, bragging to his friends and playing the primadonna, and Rockwell decided to stop using him for a while. Eventually, the boy improved his manner and resumed posing with a bit more humility. Billy Paine died at age 13, when he fell from a second-story window.

For $25 a month, Norman Rockwell had rented the second floor of George Lischke's barn for a studio at 40 Prospect Street, and installed heat, electricity, plumbing, and a large north window. The Lischkes' younger boy, Franklin, was one of Rockwell's favorite models. Between the years 1921 and 1928, Franklin posed for at least sixteen cover paintings and story illustrations. His pay rose from 50 to 75 cents per hour, and eventually he was promoted to Rockwell's "studio boy" at $5.00 a week. His responsibilities included sweeping up the studio, running errands, and occasionally answering the phone to say that Rockwell was out when the artist was pressing to meet a deadline.

Franklin Lischke was also on hand to help with the delivery of props to the studio. These could be small items—a straw basket or saxophone, perhaps—or they could be quite substantial in size. It was not unfamiliar to see a buggy, sofa, or doghouse moved up the flight of stairs to the studio. For a painting of a policeman on duty, Rockwell hauled a motorcycle up to the second floor. Carrying the cycle down the stairs proved to be a greater ordeal than bringing it up. Midway in the effort Rockwell lost his grip and

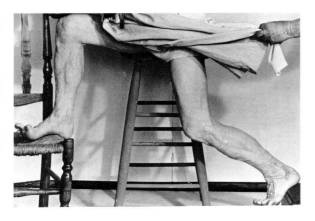

A long stride captured mid-air was difficult enough to pose for two or three minutes of photography. Holding a position such as this for twenty minutes at a stretch, however, could be a real test of stamina. Such was the exertion required when Rockwell painted from life during his years in New Rochelle.

let it go. The motorcycle flopped down the stairs, broke through the closed door at the landing, and piled itself into a heap at the doorstep.

Even small props could prove troublesome, however. Young Franklin was instructed to purchase a couple of trout at a neighborhood fish store for a painting of a farmer fishing from a pier. It was an unusually hot day for working, and particularly unsavory for painting dead fish. "Frank," Rockwell called out after a few hours, "I can't stand the smell of these fish a moment longer. Put them in your mother's refrigerator and I'll finish painting them tomorrow." Mrs. Lischke nearly fainted when she opened the refrigerator that evening and ordered her son to return the pair to Rockwell immediately. After the painting was completed the next day, Rockwell told Franklin to bury the fish in the back yard. The boy must not have made a deep enough hole, because some cats dug up the foul-smelling prop and deposited the bones gratefully at Rockwell's doorstep.

In a gesture of discretion, Rockwell advised the young teenager to stay away from the studio one day while he painted a model posing in a provocative one-piece bathing suit. Franklin happened to spot the attractive female as she entered the building, and he could not resist a peek at her in costume. He climbed a shaky ladder at the back of the studio and peered through the window from the top rung. Observing the young man from the corner of his eye, Rockwell quietly walked over to the window and drew the shade. In Franklin's haste to withdraw from the scene, he jumped from midway down the ladder, making an awful clatter as he dropped to the ground, and was too embarrassed to show up the next day.

The trials and tribulations of using young children made for amusing tales told years later. The older teenagers—also an important subject category for Rockwell's covers—were drawn from a more reliable source: a group of students attending New Rochelle High School. This group was sufficiently ample to service the entire community of New Rochelle artists and illustrators. Jackie James Walker recalls that modeling for the several artists in the immediate vicinity provided a steady means of earning pocket money for her and her friends. For them posing was as commonplace an activity as baby sitting.

Of all the New Rochelle artists, "Mr. Rockwell" was the most desirable. His studio was not like the other cluttered, rather gloomy garrets; Rockwell's was airy, light, and orderly. Rockwell also paid more than the others. But most of all, Rockwell made posing fun for them. "He had such a fine sense of humor," Jackie James Walker recalled. "He made the hours pass pleasantly."

Rockwell's covers were more ambitious than the simple sketches executed by the other less notable artists in the community. These covers required hours of posing. The chore of sitting still for long periods was made enjoyable by the artist's lighthearted talk and his easy manner of including his subjects in the planning process. He posed each subject separately, in costume and with props, but made a point of first describing the overall concept from the small drawing, then sharing each stage of the painting at the periodic intervals when the model was relaxing from the pose.

Posing adults presented its own set of difficulties for the New Rochelle illustrator. As long as Rockwell painted from life, he was obliged to find someone who could afford the time to pose. Working directly from a model, Rockwell figured the process of drawing the figure in charcoal on the canvas, then painting over the drawing in oil generally took three days to complete a single figure, sometimes longer. Consequently, he required the services of professional models. In New Rochelle it was fairly easy to hire a professional for two or three days, an unemployed actor perhaps, or a professional living nearby or working at the Art Students League in the city. There were favorites, of course, and the illustrators might have to make arrangements with each other to reserve a particular model in time for an impending deadline. Naturally, Rockwell had his own favorites that suited his themes and he used them over and over, posing them in a variety of ways to avoid monotony as much as possible. And if he was lucky, he could find a model no other illustrator had yet used.

Such was the case with James K. Van Brunt, five foot two inches tall, bearing the finest mustache Norman Rockwell had ever seen. "What a face!" Rockwell reported, "And all mine, I gloated, all mine. That knobby nose, thick and square at the end with a bump in the middle; those big, sad, dog eyes which, however, burned with a fierce, warlike sparkle; that mustache. And all crammed together in a small, narrow head so that if you glanced at him quickly that was all you saw—eyes, nose, and mustache."

As it turned out, the face was somewhat *too* distinct and after Van Brunt appeared on three *Post* covers, editor Horace Lorimer objected. The public would get bored if exposed to the same face too frequently, he insisted. Rockwell was distressed by the thought of losing his favorite model and urged Van Brunt to shave off the mustache so that he could use the old man again. At first Van Brunt's pride caused him to refuse the offer, but two weeks later he agreed to shave it off in exchange for ten dollars. Once the mustache was removed, Rockwell was even more distressed: "Mr. Van Brunt's lower lip stuck out beyond his upper lip by about an inch and was just as identifying as the mustache," he lamented. In order to disguise Van Brunt, Rockwell conceived of ways to paint the old man by concealing the upper lip and hiding the mouth altogether: "But it got to be more of a chore and worry than the mustache. I couldn't go on painting pictures of an old man with the lower third of his face hidden behind his hands or a book or his hat." Exasperated, Rockwell finally told Van Brunt to grow back the mustache. But his advanced age (by now he was over eighty years old) must have diminished his hirsute powers. The mustache "never attained its former sweeping plumpness, its majestic swoop at the ends." Never without kindness, Rockwell endowed his favorite model with an even grander

Couple in Carriage. Saturday Evening Post cover, September 19, 1925.

mustache, exaggerating its shape and density in his painting. "I faked the mustache bigger and fuller to please him. I did the same in the next two." When he found he was again using Van Brunt too frequently, he used Van Brunt's figure only, having him pose in ladies' costumes. Rockwell remembered the old man prancing around the studio in an old maid's outfit, lifting the long skirt and curtsying. Only a few months after Rockwell painted Van Brunt again (his hand over the mustache), the old man died.

Like Van Brunt, Harry Seal was a favorite model Rockwell could use only occasionally because of his readily identifiable figure. Seal was rotund, with a jolly round face and thin small arms and legs. ("Someone once said he looked like a turtle," Rockwell reported.) Harry Seal had once been extremely wealthy, holding a half-interest in the Royal Baking Powder Company until the money ran out, when he became a model at the Art Students League. But he continued to live high ("I can resist anything but temptation," he had boasted) and Rockwell obtained optimum results when he pepped up Seal with a shot of whiskey. After using Harry Seal in three covers in one year, Lorimer again objected and Rockwell had to give him up for the *Post*, continuing to use him periodically for ads only.

Although Rockwell's most frequent themes involved youth and old age, he also took on an occasional period piece in those days. For these themes Rockwell preferred James Wilson, a former actor, who seemed to come to life in a costume. "He looked like a caricature of an old-time English ham actor, a nineteenth century Hamlet," Rockwell observed. He was English and he owned several costumes himself, carrying some of them about with him in an old Gladstone bag. Rockwell remembered that he had a magnificent Catholic cardinal's costume, for example. Wilson provided for his entire family by posing for artists. He worked all day and far into the night, shopped for food, and supported his two grown sons who were striving to be artists. He was intensely proud of his profession as a model, flatly refusing to pose for photography because he regarded it as degrading. He was competitive with another of his professional colleagues at the League, Pop Fredericks. Each claimed he could pose for longer hours than the other, a competition that was abandoned because it ultimately proved too fatiguing to both models and artists alike.

As he posed for Rockwell, Wilson would tell the artist one story after another about his days as an actor. It happened that many professional models were young or unsuccessful actors, capable of holding the most extraordinary facial expressions. Pop Fredericks was a former actor, and so was Edward Van Vechtan.

As the years passed, Norman Rockwell's work continued to mature. By the early 1930s he was among the most highly sought after illustrators in the country. He had remarried in 1930 and lived in a handsome home on Lord Kichener Road. In Mary Barstow, Rockwell felt he had found a real friend, "And I guess it saved me," he said.

When Rockwell painted from life, he posed the figures in the appropriate setting and costume. If props were needed, the illustrator went to the effort of obtaining them for the modeling session, regardless of how cumbersome such a project might be. This romantic pose in a surrey happened to be one Franklin Lischke particularly enjoyed holding for the considerable length of time Rockwell required. Photo United Press International.

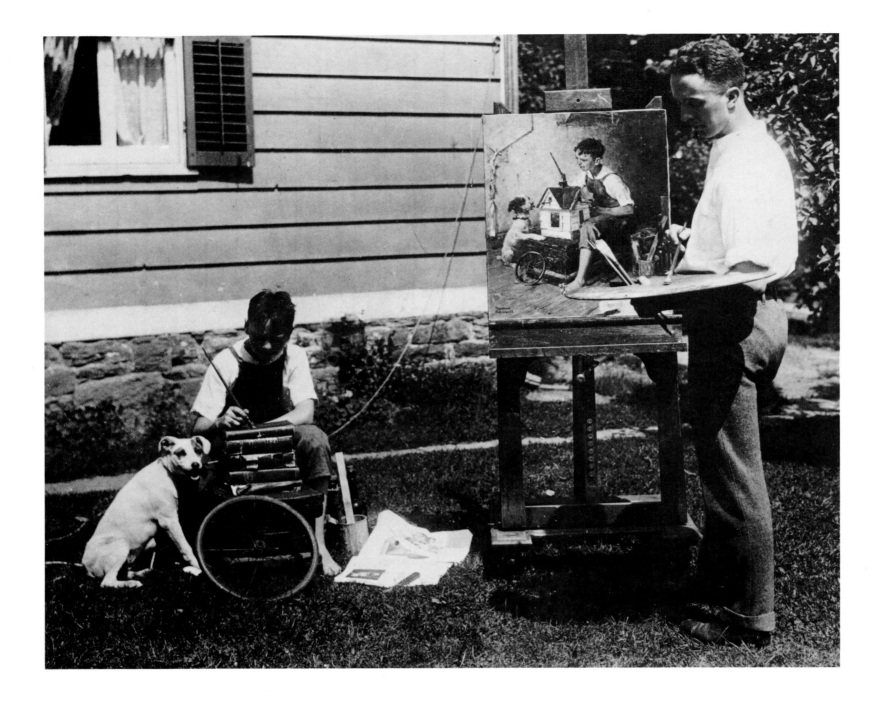

Norman
Rockwell

Clyde
Forsythe

I might have gone under without it. Because a few months after our marriage I began to have trouble with my work. Now that I was settled again and happy, the frenzied life I'd been leading before the divorce, the divorce itself, and the lonely, rootless months in New York fell in on me like a ton of bricks. While I'd been living all that, caught up in it, I'd somehow, without knowing it, kept my work apart. Some inner defense had prevented it from reaching my work and tearing that down with the rest, so that though I had been miserable I had always had my work to hang onto. It had been the one sane element in my life. But now that it had brought me through, saved me, it collapsed.

Feelings of indecision and low self-confidence nagged at Rockwell. Mary, Norman, and their eight-month-old son took off to France for eight months to see whether a new environment would make a difference. Letters written by Mary Rockwell to her family from Paris indicate that these were trying times (see *Appendix*) and it was not until Rockwell returned to the States—where he "stuck to the easel like a leech"—that he worked his way through the crisis. "Even now," he said, "I don't understand really what caused the trouble or how I gradually worked through it."

Shortly after returning from Paris, Mary gave birth to son Tom, and two years later Peter was born. The Rockwells lived well, employed a cook and a nursemaid, traveled frequently, and socialized with other illustrators in New Rochelle and in New York City. But Rockwell's restlessness grew more intense. Many of his favorite models had grown up, disappeared, or passed away, and he was working with a newer crop of professionals. A younger breed of illustrator—contemporary artists like John Falter, Stevan Dohanos, and Al Parker—was creating work that forced him to question his own pictures. And for some time the Rockwells had been troubled by the demanding social pressures that were distracting and unsatisfying. A change was in order, a fresh environment that would provide the material and tranquility needed to make pictures.

Rockwell was no fisherman, but the Batten Kill River sounded very attractive to him when his friend Fred Hildebrandt described it. Hildebrandt was a model in great demand by the New Rochelle illustrators—a fine bone structure and figure that made him an ideal pirate, hero, romantic figure, or a Yankee Doodle. Fred Hildebrandt had become so valuable to Rockwell, in fact, that the illustrator had hired him as a handyman and used him to track down props and costumes as well. They became good friends. And Hildebrandt loved two things: women and fishing. He urged Rockwell to explore the area around the Batten Kill River in Vermont. You didn't have to be a fisherman to see the virtues of the scenic river.

Franklin Lischke was the son of Norman Rockwell's landlord, George Lischke. From the elder Lischke, Rockwell rented a second-story space and converted it into a studio. It was here that young Franklin posed for the illustrator and helped him with chores around the studio. Photos Franklin Lischke.

No Swimming. Original oil painting for a *Saturday Evening Post* cover, June 4, 1921. Estate of Norman Rockwell.

No doubt Rockwell was doing a kind of self-portrait when he painted the scrawny boy lifting weights for a *Post* cover posed by Franklin Lischke, because this is how he perceived himself at that age. Staying in shape was certainly a prerequisite for posing when it came to the more active scenes. Nothing demanded greater stamina than posing live in a running position, for example. Franklin Lischke also posed for *Pilgrim's Progress* and for *No Swimming* (the skinny kid in the center; Nicholas Yager was the chubby boy at the right). Even sixty years later, Lischke remembered the difficulties involved in holding these poses: half-sitting on the edge of a low stool, his legs and feet were propped up by stacks of books, a position he had to hold for twenty minutes at a stretch. In later years, photography would simplify this arduous task, reducing a typical modeling session from three hours to a total of twenty minutes, perhaps. 🍎

Champ. Saturday Evening Post cover, April 29, 1922.

A *Pilgrim's Progress*. Original oil painting for *Life* cover, November 17, 1921. Courtesy Judy and Alan Goffman Fine Art, Blue Bell, Pennsylvania.

Sneezing Spy. Saturday Evening Post cover, October 1, 1921.

Self-Photographer. Original oil painting for a *Saturday Evening Post* cover, April 18, 1925. Courtesy Judy and Alan Goffman Fine Art, Blue Bell, Pennsylvania.

Kept In. Saturday Evening Post cover, June 10, 1922.

The Rivals. Saturday Evening Post cover, September 9, 1922.

The son of Rockwell's landlord, Franklin Lischke was, as Rockwell described him,

a narrow-shouldered, stringy adolescent with a round head. He was one of the most gullible kids I've ever known . . . his ability to digest fantastic stories was immense. Clyde [Forsythe] used to tell him the most atrocious things. He'd sit in the big armchair rubbing his knees and gulping it all in. Then he'd dash downstairs to tell his father, and later on Mr. Lischke would laugh about it with us. Franklin was an awful nice little boy and a good model. We always used to kid him because just after he was born his other brother George had looked in the cradle and said, "What is it?"

From the first job as a model in 1921, young Franklin continued to pose for Rockwell for fifteen other assignments until 1928, and he proved to be an excellent kid to have around the studio for odd jobs. As a result of his sustained relationship with Norman Rockwell, Lischke wound up being an illustrator himself. "He was the best thing that could have happened to me," maintained Lischke nearly sixty years later. 🦋

In Need of Sympathy. Original oil painting for a *Saturday Evening Post* cover, October 2, 1926. Courtesy Danenberg Gallery.

Moonlight Serenade. Saturday Evening Post cover, August 30, 1924.

Couple Striding. Saturday Evening Post cover, May 5, 1928.

Rockwell got along well with John L. Malone, a pleasant, white-haired model he used often. Malone would read aloud to the illustrator while posing. He could read as long as eight hours at a clip and he read Rockwell's favorites: Balzac, Turgenev, Tolstoy, De Maupassant. ❦

James Wilson was the best costume model Rockwell ever had. A former actor, Wilson carried his own costumes around in a black satchel and while he posed would talk for hours about his years in the theater. "He'd darn near kill you with his memories," Rockwell recalled. ❦

Dave Campion, who owned a newsstand in New Rochelle, was a favorite model for Rockwell. Although he wasn't a professional, he managed to spend the length of time required for posing. Rockwell was grateful for this because Campion's lean physique was a type he liked to use frequently in his work. Campion posed with Pop Fredericks and Bill Sundermeyer for the Christmas carollers. According to Rockwell, "Dave Campion couldn't play the violin, nor could Pop Fredericks play anything. Bill Sundermeyer had no ear for music." ❦

LEFT TOP: *Storekeeper Modeling Lady's Hat. Saturday Evening Post* cover, May 3, 1924. LEFT MIDDLE: *Principal and Graduate. Saturday Evening Post* cover, June 26, 1926. LEFT BOTTOM: *Man Threading Needle.* Original oil painting for a *Saturday Evening Post* cover, April 8, 1922, and advertisement for Interwoven, Division of Kayser Roth Corporation. Courtesy Judy and Alan Goffman Fine Art, Blue Bell, Pennsylvania. BELOW: *Valet Admiring a Sock.* Original oil painting for an advertisement for Interwoven, Division of Kayser Roth Corporation. Courtesy Judy and Alan Goffman Fine Art, Blue Bell, Pennsylvania.

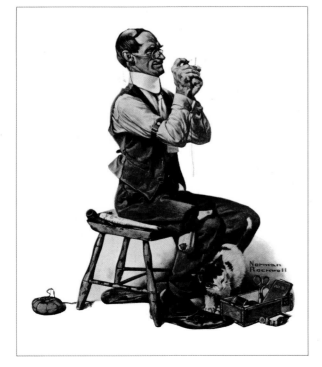

Christmas Caroling Trio. Original oil painting for a *Saturday Evening Post* cover, December 8, 1923. Estate of Norman Rockwell.

Steamship Comfort. Saturday Evening Post cover, September 8, 1923.

Fishing in Comfort. Saturday Evening Post cover, July 19, 1930.

Many professional models started out as actors and came to modeling because they had failed or retired. Like James Wilson, Pop Fredericks was an actor who claimed that he was "cheated of his fame" when he was replaced on Broadway in *Abie's Irish Rose* only after the play became popular, others receiving credit for the role *he* had originated. Fredericks was a model for the Art Students League in New York City, and would come out to New Rochelle frequently to pose for the illustrators there. He took great pride in his modeling profession, but he clearly preferred the relaxed poses befitting his age and volume. Even if he should fall asleep as he posed in a comfortable chair, Fredericks would expect to be awakened at the end of twenty minutes so that "he could rest."

Dancing to a Cello. Saturday Evening Post cover, February 3, 1923.

Dancing Couple. Original oil painting for a *Saturday Evening Post* cover, December 8, 1928. Courtesy Judy and Alan Goffman Fine Art, Blue Bell, Pennsylvania.

Chivalry. Original painting for a *Saturday Evening Post* cover, February 16, 1929. Courtesy Judy and Alan Goffman Fine Art, Blue Bell, Pennsylvania.

Rockwell forced himself to use Harry Seal sparingly. His rotund shape was so distinctive that *Post* editor Lorimer would object to the obvious repetition if Rockwell used Seal too frequently. A model at the Art Students League like Pop Fredericks, Seal was a gentleman, "well bred and polite," and the illustrator enjoyed using him. Rockwell told the story about Seal posing for the painting called *Chivalry* when Seal happened to doze off during the session.

He was portraying a man who had fallen asleep over a book and I guess he was living the part off and on. Suddenly he started. "I'm getting faint," he said, glancing wildly about. "You haven't a drop of whiskey somewhere?" I ran into the house and brought out a bottle. He drank a shot. "Ahh," he said, "s'better, better. That was a near thing, Mr. Rockwell, a near thing." So every day after that he'd suddenly feel faint and I'd have to revive him with a shot of whiskey. ☙

Card Tricks. Original oil painting for a *Saturday Evening Post* cover, March 22, 1930. Courtesy Judy and Alan Goffman Fine Art, Blue Bell, Pennsylvania.

The Dispute. Original oil painting for advertisement for the *Encyclopedia Britannica*. Courtesy Martin Diamond Fine Arts, New York.

Bum Cooking Sausage. Saturday Evening Post cover, October 18, 1924.

Crossword Puzzle. Saturday Evening Post cover, January 31, 1925.

The Phrenologist. *Saturday Evening Post* cover, March 27, 1926.

Browsing Among Used Books. *Saturday Evening Post* cover, August 14, 1926.

Painting Tavern Sign. Original oil painting for a *Saturday Evening Post* cover, February 6, 1926. Courtesy Martin Diamond Fine Arts, New York.

The sequence of events leading to the unfortunate outcome in the life of James K. Van Brunt is fully documented in Rockwell's illustrations. Van Brunt was a favorite of Rockwell's throughout the 1920s. He was a dedicated model, would practice his poses in front of the mirror in advance of a session, and try to convince the illustrator that his ideas for the pose were better than Rockwell's. He'd been through a great deal in his lifetime, had fought the Indians, was a veteran of the Civil and Spanish-American Wars. But this distinguished, ninety-eight-pound gentleman (who normally dressed in a frock coat, waist coat, and high silk hat) went through one of the most humiliating ordeals in his life as Rockwell's model.

His pride and joy was his glorious mustache, the single feature that made him superior to all other models.

Rockwell loved the mustache, too, depicted it with a particular flourish each time, but Horace Lorimer was quick to size up the situation. He demanded that Rockwell discontinue his use of the model with the bushy mustache before the *Post* readers got bored with it. With a good deal of friendly coercion and a $10 check, Rockwell succeeded in persuading Van Brunt to shave off his glorious mustache. And for the first *Post* cover ever to be printed in full color (not in the old-fashioned red-and-black ink), Rockwell used the shorn Van Brunt as a model. Alas, the strange configuration of Van Brunt's upper lip was even more conspicuous than the mustache had been. In the next two Van Brunt covers, therefore, Rockwell was obliged to conceal the unsightly feature the best he could. 🐦

Cowboy Listening to Records. Saturday Evening Post cover, August 13, 1927.

The sad saga of James K. Van Brunt continued after the stupendous mustache was shaved off. Rockwell could no longer continue to devise methods of concealing Van Brunt's unfortunate upper lip. Exasperated, Rockwell suggested Van Brunt grow back his mustache. But all was not repaired. Even without shaving for a considerable period of time, the elderly Van Brunt was incapable of restoring his mustache to its original splendor, no matter how much he encouraged it with regular preening. Van Brunt was simply too old to re-create his abundant whiskers. Rockwell felt so much compassion for the man that in the following two *Post* covers he went out of his way to exaggerate the size of the meager mustache, making it bigger and fuller than life. It wasn't easy to continue using Van Brunt under these conditions, so Rockwell had to concoct another way to make the best of his best model. Finally, he had the ingenious idea of posing Van Brunt as three old maids in the next cover, careful to avoid any suggestion of a single whisker. In his final Van Brunt cover, painted only a few months before the old man died of a respiratory ailment, Rockwell concealed the mustache for the last time.

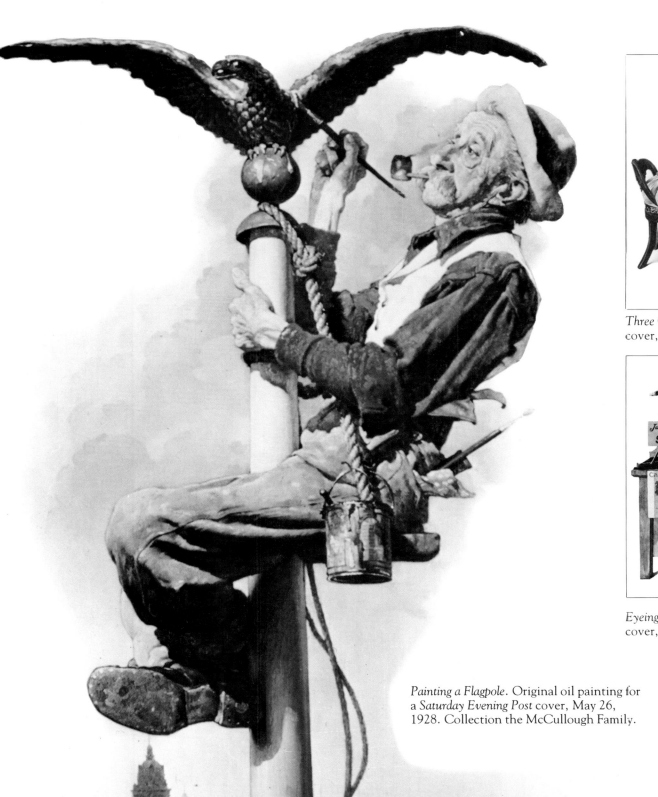

Painting a Flagpole. Original oil painting for a *Saturday Evening Post* cover, May 26, 1928. Collection the McCullough Family.

Three Gossips. Saturday Evening Post cover, January 12, 1929.

Eyeing a Sax. Saturday Evening Post cover, November 2, 1929.

YANKEE DOODLE CAME TO TOWN · RIDING ON A PONY

Home from Vacation. Original oil painting for a *Saturday Evening Post* cover, September 13, 1930. Collection Mr. and Mrs. Phil Grace.

Colonial Couple. Saturday Evening Post cover, July 25, 1931.

CK A FEATHER IN HIS HAT · AND CALLED IT MACARONI

Yankee Doodle. Mural for the Nassau Tavern, Princeton, New Jersey, 1937. © Princeton Municipal Improvement, Inc.

Lean and lithe, athletic and handsome: that was Fred Hildebrandt, a favorite model for several of the New Rochelle illustrators. He could be an ideal Yankee Doodle, an adventurer, or a romantic lover, receiving proposals in marriage from women dazzled by his pictures. Hildebrandt was a good friend to Rockwell, helped him with odd jobs when he could, and traveled with him to the west coast. According to Rockwell, Hildebrandt kissed three women as he posed for the *Post* cover published July 25, 1931. The first he kissed in New Rochelle where the cover was begun, the second in Chicago, and the third in Hollywood as the illustrator and model made a westward trip together. ❦

The Hunter. Saturday Evening Post cover, November 16, 1935.

Arlington
FRIENDSHIP AND HARD WORK

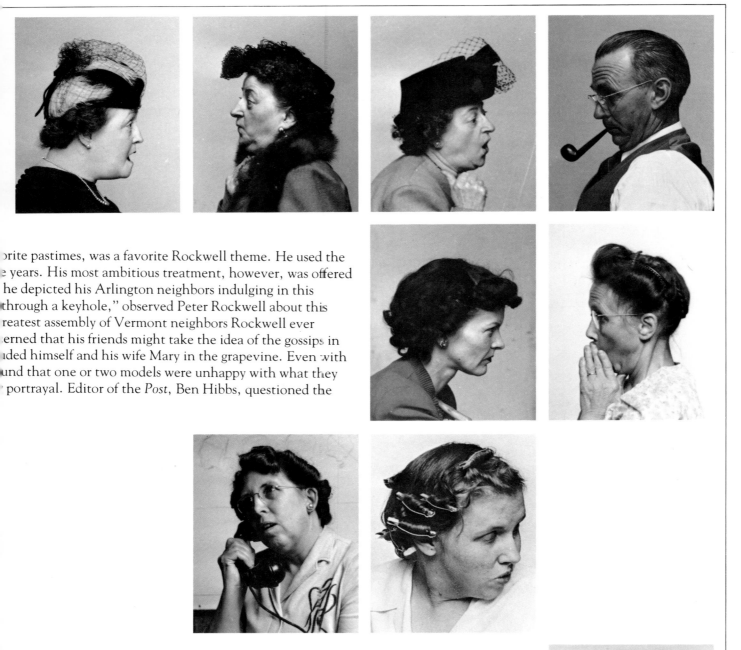

orite pastimes, was a favorite Rockwell theme. He used the
e years. His most ambitious treatment, however, was offered
he depicted his Arlington neighbors indulging in this
through a keyhole," observed Peter Rockwell about this
reatest assembly of Vermont neighbors Rockwell ever
erned that his friends might take the idea of the gossips in
ded himself and his wife Mary in the grapevine. Even with
und that one or two models were unhappy with what they
portrayal. Editor of the *Post*, Ben Hibbs, questioned the

uthenticity of the faces. Only when Rockwell showed him the photographs he had taken of
he models was Hibbs convinced the illustrator had not imagined these types: they were real!
  Only twelve of the fifteen gossips have been positively identified by Arlington neighbors.
"There are a few in here from Manchester," offered Clara Edgerton.) From left to right, the
rst is unknown, then onto Mrs. Comar, to Mrs. Jessie Harrington, to Jessie Harrington
lso in *Ration Board* and son of a "charwoman"), to Jenny McKee (the other
harwoman), to an unknown gossip, to Rena Crofut, to Mary Rockwell, to
oris Crofut (Rena Crofut's daughter), to Lester Brush (of *Facts of Life*), to
rs. George Zimmer, to another unknown gossip, to George Zimmer, to Frank Hall,
ompleting the circle with the illustrator himself.

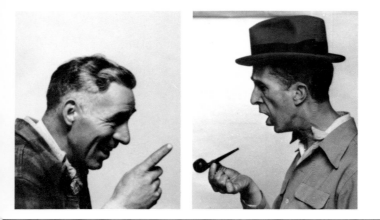

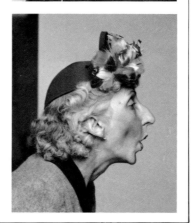

"*Don't Say I Said It!*". *Life* magazine cover, March 23, 1922.

Gossip, as one of America's fav
subject more than once over th
in his 1948 *Post* cover in which
popular activity. "Like looking
painting. It was just about the g
gathered in a single work. Conc
the wrong spirit, Rockwell incl
this precaution, however, he fo
regarded as a rather unflattering

a
t

(
f
(
c
L
M
c

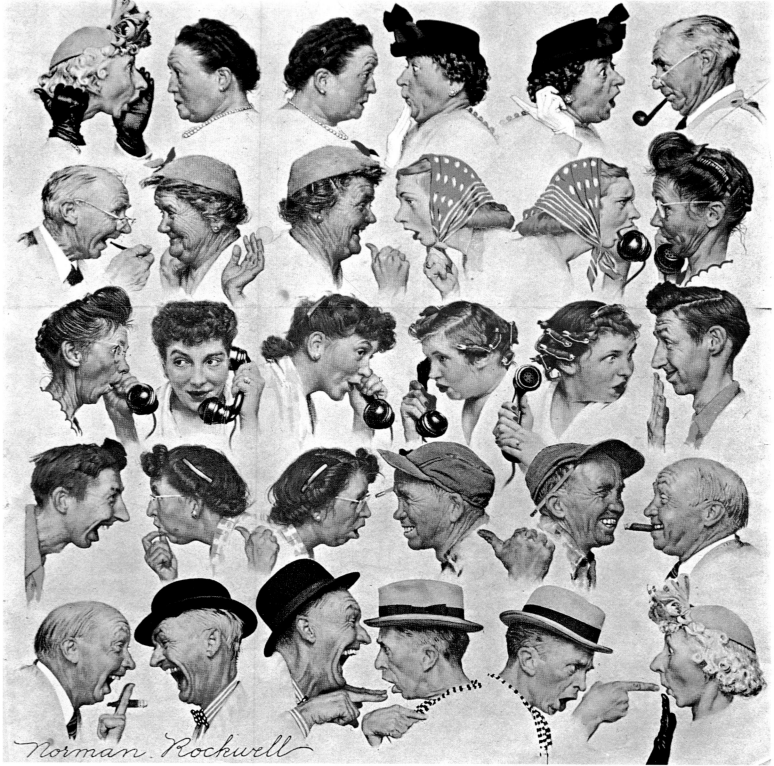

The Gossips. Original oil painting for a *Saturday Evening Post* cover, March 6, 1948.

A s it happened, Fred Hildebrandt was absolutely correct about the virtues of the Batten Kill River. The river flows through Arlington, Vermont, weaving its way through a clump of mountains that form one of the most attractive sites in southern Vermont. The Arlington realtor Burton Immen arranged for the Rockwells to purchase a white clapboard farmhouse and sixty acres of land along the bank of the river. Over the winter of 1938 the Rockwells had one of the two barns on the property converted into a studio and the family spent the following summer in their new home. The environment seemed so right that Mary and Norman winterized the house and took up year-round residence the following year.

It seems extraordinary that four illustrators for the *Saturday Evening Post* managed to wind up in a community of only 1600 people. Besides Rockwell there were Mead Schaeffer and Jack Atherton, with George Hughes arriving later. Their presence provided a unique kind of fellowship. Mead Schaeffer and his wife Elizabeth were especially close to the Rockwells. ("This friendship with Schaef—a working illustrator, someone who shared my ideals, understood my problems—stimulated me. I guess it helped my work almost as much as moving to Arlington.") To this group, in 1948, was added the other Schafers—Chris and his wife Mary—who had come to a rural way of life from North Shore Drive in Chicago. Chris Schafer became Rockwell's business manager, a function he continued to serve even after the Rockwells moved to Stockbridge, Massachusetts, in 1953.

The Rockwells' first home in Arlington was located on a secluded back road along the river. From 1939 until 1943 Norman Rockwell worked in the converted barn, situated about one hundred feet from the house. In 1943, not long after Rockwell had completed his *Four Freedoms*, the studio burned to the ground in the middle of the night. "We kids were all down with the measles," recalled the youngest son Peter, "and we watched the fire from the living room until dawn. We were so carried away by the aura of those great flames licking the rooftops that we almost hoped our house would catch on fire too, just to prolong the excitement. It was an amazing sight." The fire destroyed many cherished items—paintings, sketches, costumes, antiques, photographic records, the accumulation of twenty-eight years of painting, traveling, and collecting. "It's like losing your left arm," Rockwell said, "and waking up in the middle of the night and reaching out for a glass of water and suddenly realizing that you haven't got anything to reach with."

The shock of the fire, combined with the Rockwells' desire for a less secluded home, resulted in an immediate decision to buy a house a few miles away on West Arlington's village green. ("Rockwell was like that," said Chris Schafer. "He'd make up his mind to do something and that was it—it was done the same morning.")

Their second house stood only fifty feet from a twin Greek revival home that was occupied by dairy farmer Jim Edgerton, his wife Clara, and their four children, Edith, Joy, Buddy, and Ardis. Beyond the front porch of the Rockwell home stood the covered bridge spanning the Batten Kill, a one-room schoolhouse, a dance pavilion, and a New England church with an attached community hall. This environment had much to offer. The school was no longer in use, so Rockwell converted it into a temporary studio until Walt Squires, the carpenter, completed construction of the new Rockwell studio. (Buddy Edgerton remembers that the bulldozer that came to break ground for the studio was the first he'd ever beheld, because it was a machine not seen frequently during the war.)

Several years later Rockwell invited six art students—Don Winslow, Don Spaulding, William McBride, Robert Hogue, Harold Stevenson, and Jim Gaboda—to work under his tutelage, offering the schoolhouse for dormitory living and studio. After that summer of 1950 Don Winslow continued to live in the schoolhouse for several more years.

On the green were also located the dance pavilion and the grange hall where Norman Rockwell enjoyed square dancing regularly. ("He could go all night and never puff a bit," Mead Schaeffer noted.) These places, so accessible to the artist, made living on the village green most amiable.

The move to Arlington gave Rockwell a real lift. His temperament was ideally suited to the New England reserve surrounding him. Although he was known to be cordial, he had chosen to withdraw from the whirling social and professional pressures of New York, and he was not eager to replace that with other kinds of pressures a small town might impose. Needing solitude, Rockwell appreciated the civil but reserved manner of the native Vermonter. "The people we met were rugged and self-contained," he remarked. "None of that sham 'I am *so* glad to know you!' accompanied by radiant smiles. They shook my hand, said, 'How do,' and waited to see how I'd turn out. Not hostile but reserved with a dignity and personal integrity which are rare in suburbia, where you're familiar with someone before you know him. In Vermont you earn the right to be called by your first name."

Rockwell had said it takes twenty years for a Vermonter to accept you as one of them. Others might say it's never possible: "There are two classes of people who aren't natives," a Vermonter explained to one of Rockwell's

Photos © 1981 Susan E. Meyer

My Studio Burns. Old Corn House Collection, Stockbridge, Massachusetts. During their fourteen years in Arlington, the Rockwells lived in two different homes situated along the picturesque Batten Kill River. After an unfortunate fire destroyed Rockwell's studio and its contents in 194_ (described with the illustrator's characteristic humor in the drawing shown right), the Rockwells purchased a house on the West Arlington green. Here they lived only a few feet from a twin house owned by the Edgerton family

My Studio burns

by Norman Rockwell

Tommy in pajamas gives the alarm 1:15 a.m.

Wow !!!!

light and phone connection burned out

Off for the Fire Department

Here they come !!!

Jerry, Tommy and Peter watch

by the way, the kids were having the measles

Fire Chief Safford sings "It aint gunna rain no more"

Med Grover square dances gets thrown

Family bicycles rescued

Everyone enjoys Spectacle 2 a.m.

Coffee and sandwiches till 5:30 a.m.

By the dawn's early light

Norman Rockwell

us 7 a.m.

friends: "There are summer people and there are year-round summer people." For someone like Norman Rockwell, this freedom from social expectations represented a comfortable change from the whirl in New Rochelle, and a welcome atmosphere for work.

In Vermont Rockwell found the environment he needed to concentrate totally on his pictures, a quiet and stable schedule for painting. What he also found was a community whose way of life most closely approximated the scenes he painted, a rural atmosphere where living is more clearly rooted to the universal themes associated with growing up and growing old. Rockwell didn't have to search far for ideas and subjects: they were all around him in Vermont. "It was like living in another world," he said. "A more honest one somehow. Because almost everyone had lived in the town all his life and had known one another since childhood and even everybody's parents and grandparents, there could be little pretension. And because farming was a hard life and yet not competitive, there was great neighborliness.... The pressures were very strong, not toward conformity, but toward decency and honesty." This was the world Norman Rockwell had depicted long before he had laid eyes on Arlington, Vermont. For the next fifteen years he would feel at home living in this world.

If the tempo and style of living suited him, the way he adapted his methods of working to this environment were equally beneficial. All around him were potential subjects for his paintings. Whenever he stepped out of his studio he was likely to encounter a "type," a natural and characteristic face for his pictures. With the exception of Fred Hildebrandt, who came to Arlington to pose for Rockwell from time to time, the illustrator no longer relied on professionals for posing. Instead he turned entirely to those living around him. "Now my pictures grew out of the world around me, the everyday life of my neighbors. I didn't fake anymore." All of this was made possible by Rockwell's use of the camera.

Until he moved to Arlington he had used photography as little as possible. Once, as early as 1921, he did use a camera, when he prepared a cover for *American* magazine. Inside the issue appeared a description of this cover: "Since he could not ask any boy to hold a yawn long enough for him to draw it, Mr. Rockwell went himself to a photographer and registered before the camera. In other words, Mr. Rockwell is his own model, so far as the yawn goes." But he continued to use photography only occasionally, "trying to hang onto at least the shreds of my self-respect," he said, until he was unable to resist the advantages that became more and more evident to him. A photographer came to help about 1937, but even then illustrations were painted from living models and from photographs. In the beginning, he used photographs for dogs and children only and was no longer forced to ask models to pose for long hours. Then came the pressure from the magazines to adopt different angles, new viewpoints into his work, as younger artists such as Stevan Dohanos were doing. No longer limited to the simple, head-on view from his easel, Rockwell could depict a scene viewed from above, or from near the floor.

The photographs relieved Rockwell of a great deal of tension in working. He no longer had to paint frantically against the clock, commanding his models to check their poses for long hours. Professional models were the only ones who could afford the time necessary for posing, and they were accustomed to holding expressions and poses for an extended period of time without fatiguing. With photography he could snap a spontaneous expression, could choose from among a variety of expressions, could record an awkward pose instantaneously. He also found he could be less literal in painting from photographs. "Working from the model, I had found it impossible to paint a green sweater from a red sweater. It sounds silly, but I just hadn't been able to do it. So I'd had to hunt up the right sweater in green. A nuisance. When working with photographs, I seem to be able to recompose in many ways, in form, tone, and color."

In New Rochelle, Rockwell's stable of models was necessarily limited by the number of models available to him under the demanding conditions required for posing. In Arlington, Rockwell discovered dozens of models who could suit his purposes. He found them everywhere—in the general store, square dancing at the grange hall, driving along the road, in the post office. Arlington had as many types as the artist had ideas.

The range of subjects and their treatment expanded greatly in Vermont, partly because Rockwell had a greater range from which to select. He felt unable to contrive. He singled out the characters most closely associated with the topics of his paintings: *The Story Teller*, for example, shows a marine sitting in a cluttered garage, retelling war stories to attentive neighbors. For this idea Rockwell selected Benedict's Garage in Arlington as the setting, and used both Benedict brothers (and a young man who had recently returned from the marines) in the garage to pose for the painting. For a cover involving a sheriff, Rockwell selected Arlington's sheriff Harvey McKee; for a country doctor he called on Arlington's own Dr. Russell. The strong kinship Americans felt for the personalities depicted in Rockwell's work derived, in large part, from the authenticity of the subjects themselves; they were real. In a sense, Rockwell was a realist; he happened to view the American way of life with constantly renewing optimism, but he drew from genuine sources.

Rockwell's clarity of purpose was remarkable. He knew just what he wanted. It may seem strange, perhaps, that even though his imagination was consumed with a precise image, he still found it necessary to photograph. Why not paint directly from the imagination?

The fact is that Rockwell was uneasy about making up pictures "in his head," as he would say. He painted what he saw in front of him—from live models or photographs—rarely working out of his imagination alone. Although eager to entertain his youngest son Peter one evening because the

A jubilant group of Arlington citizenry enjoyed the triumph of shooting a black bear in the woods at Benedict Hollow. Jim and Clara Edgerton joined in the celebration, as did Tommy Rockwell standing alongside Jim Edgerton.

Photo courtesy Clara Edgerton.

child was ailing with some minor illness, Rockwell resisted the boy's entreaties to make some drawings. "I can't draw if I don't have a model in front of me," he explained to Peter. He finally consented only under pressure from the boy. ("Just imagine a picture and draw it for me," Peter urged.) The drawings—of clowns—were beautifully executed but not without difficulty.

Photography, as a stage in the creative process, was a key step for him, therefore: first the imagined picture, then the photographs, then the painting developed in increasing stages of specificity. In selecting props, models, and costumes, he was responding to his imagined idea, committing the realization of this idea first to film, then to canvas.

With photography Rockwell was able to reach for more complex subjects since he was no longer restricted to what he could construct in his studio. In 1942 the graphics of the *Post* cover changed, demanding more extensive treatment of the backgrounds, and the settings of Rockwell's illustrations often became as important as the characters themselves. Photography made it possible for Rockwell to shoot on location the scenes not normally accessible to him: a backyard in Troy, a train station, an empty music hall. Here he could record the accidents of light and the specific details he might have missed in sketching. He could pose the model in the actual setting or in his studio, combining the setting with the model later if he chose. With a *live* model sitting before him for several hours, the illustrator and sitter shared a relatively constant middle ground viewpoint. With the camera, Rockwell could record the scene—either totally or in part—and deal with the image from a variety of viewpoints. In *Freedom of Worship*, for example, the viewer stands in an altogether different perspective from where the artist would have stood to achieve a similar composition.

Although Rockwell knew a great deal about photography and could pull off any number of tricks in the darkroom if needed, he did not make his own photographs. He wasn't even interested at looking through the camera during a photo session. Instead, he worked with a photographer, preferably one he had trained himself. His interest was not in acquiring fine photographs, but in gathering abundant reference material, details that would reinforce the story line. In fact, Rockwell complained about a professional photographer he used once because he was *too* good. Rockwell liked photographs that were gray—in middle values only—so that he would not be led in his painting by photographic effects. He usually had three prints made for each subject—a normal print, one very dark (for highlight details), one very light (for details in dark areas), and he adjusted the values accordingly in his painting. For the same reasons he never used color photographs, preferring instead to establish his colors independently of the photograph. Photographs were taken with a 4 x 5 inch camera—generally set at f:8—and the photographer would develop the film and prints immediately after the session in the darkroom located in Rockwell's studio. The illustrator would be waiting to examine the prints early the next day so that he could get started on his painting.

The photographic session became a central part of the picture-making process for Rockwell. Mind you, this wasn't just any routine photography session: it was a stage production. Imagine the amount of preparation, the sets, the props, the costumes necessary to stage some of the scenes: Mary Rockwell might spend days searching for precisely the right object for a precise function; the handyman would construct a set in the studio with props provided by Mary; the performers would come on stage and the director would set the characters in place. Rockwell carefully explained the entire scene, showing sketches, so that the performers would "climb into" their roles. In directing the models, Rockwell would, as he described it, "discard all dignity and vanity to get into the act." Occasionally he would find a model who looked the part but couldn't lay aside his own individuality to act another part. ("What you need is an actor," Rockwell would say about his models.) So Rockwell would pose himself first, give the expression he was looking for, then request the model to do the same. Frequently he would do this over and over until he struck exactly the right pose and the right facial expression. He'd extract the best performances by demonstrating the effects he was after: a cough, a sneer, a surprised expression, arms akimbo, legs twisted into a comical position, just what was needed for the story. After some time the model inevitably found the "ham in him," losing all self-consciousness, and acting the part with genuine enthusiasm. When the models were properly whipped up, Rockwell would get excited and call out to the photographer, "ok, ok, ok, ok" gesturing wildly with his

The long, cold winters in Arlington had their redeeming moments. Here Jim Edgerton had hitched up his horse to a sleigh, in order to take the Rockwell boys on a joy ride.

Photo courtesy Clara Edgerton.

hands to indicate the timing to the man under the black cloth. "It was a real occasion," remembers Jarvis Rockwell. "He might bring a horse into the studio, or a bunch of chickens. It was like the circus had come to town. And you knew Pop was feeling good. He was at his best." Don Spaulding remembered, "You'd want to do anything for him."

"In spite of occasional vagaries I couldn't ask for better models than my neighbors," recalled Rockwell. "Or more obliging ones. I put them through hell, asking them to assume (and hold) postures that would lay out a yogi, expressions which would exhaust a mime. And they do it happily, refuse to get mad. I don't know what I'd do without them . . . . I guess if my neighbors weren't so pleasant and obliging I'd have to give up work. I couldn't do it without them."

Each session was an intense event, with many pictures taken. Often the artist discarded his idea from that session entirely, and it was hard to recall whether the image was used finally.

> My unfortunate practice of changing models in mid-picture is sometimes a source of trouble and embarrassment. I use one person, decide he's not right, and get another. But in the struggle with the picture I often forget to inform the first model that he is no longer being used. So he tells all his friends, "Wait until you see me. I'm coming out on a *Post* cover next month. You watch for it. I'm the man holding the shovel." Then the cover appears. He's not on it and is quite understandably embarrassed.

Rockwell's talent for dealing with models was not confined to the way he posed them. He developed a rapport with them; he treated them "like honored guests," Don Spaulding observed. Rockwell made them know how much he valued their work and that the success of his paintings depended on *them*. While he must have known that being selected to pose for the well known illustrator was a thrill for them, that it gave them the opportunity to see for themselves the magical process of producing a cover for the great magazine they saw each week, Rockwell was never patronizing or condescending to his models. He advised other artists to do the same: "If your models feel that you are their friend instead of their boss, and if you can make them feel that they are very important to the success of your picture, they invariably will cooperate. You cannot get people to do things for you that are difficult, no matter how much you pay them or order them about, unless they like and trust you."

Rockwell insisted on paying his models, even if they wanted to volunteer their services, and he paid them well. Other less successful illustrators admitted that Norman made it somewhat difficult for them because he paid his models so well they felt obliged to keep up with the rates. At the outset, Rockwell paid $5.00 a sitting for a child; $10.00 for an adult. Only his own

During their years in Arlington, a community of good friends surrounded the Rockwells. Their neighbor on the West Arlington green, Clara Edgerton (in the photo shown above, standing between Norman and Mary Rockwell), was a steadfast friend. For the Schaeffers and the Rockwells, just about any event was occasion for a gathering, especially Thanksgiving and Christmas. The photograph shown below was taken at such an occasion. From left to right: Peter, Tom, Jarvis, and Norman Rockwell, Patty Schaeffer, Colonel Ayres, Mary Atherton, Lee Schaeffer, Mary Rockwell, Elizabeth and Mead Schaeffer.

children earned less! Mrs. Hoyt received $15.00 when she posed for Rockwell's *Freedom of Worship*, a sum that seemed extraordinary during the war. "I had eight children in the house at that time, so $15.00 sure came in handy," she recalled. After the photographic session Rockwell would send out for Cokes for the children, thank his models earnestly, then hand them a check that had been sealed in an envelope, a gracious detail that did not go unnoticed by his colleagues.

Rockwell enjoyed having people in his studio, particularly his good friends whose advice he valued. "I'm having trouble with a painting," he might say to a friend, "and I really could use your help." Mary Schafer recalls these sessions:

> You'd troop out back to his studio and you'd give your honest opinion. Everyone was an expert in his estimation. You could say anything you wanted with no fear whatsoever. And all kinds of opinions would spring forth. We all felt we were contributing to an important thing. He'd take in all the opinions and the next day he'd do whatever he wanted to do in the first place.

"He'd ask you what you didn't like about his painting in progress, and he'd watch your face while you studied it," remembers Don Spaulding. "If you didn't get the story *right away* he knew something was wrong."

Every detail in the painting was organized to support the story, a feature that is particularly critical for a magazine cover. "He had a passion for detail," said Peter Rockwell. "And every detail had to be right." When he was planning a painting, he was amazingly observant: the marvelous legs on the Brushes' Victorian piano prompted him to borrow the two-thousand-pound instrument for two weeks. That ceramic pitcher he noticed last week—did it belong to Mrs. Marsh or Mrs. Whalen? He once came to a screeching halt in his car when he spotted precisely the rump he needed for a female figure. The next day the young woman appeared at his studio at 8 o'clock, summoned by the eager illustrator, and proud to be of service.

As his work matured, he became even more insistent on the precise details to be photographed. David Loveless, a printmaker in Stockbridge, remembered a time that Rockwell was so determined to have a model clothed in a specific dress that he had Loveless print an exact imagined paisley pattern on a piece of fabric. The printed fabric was then given to a dressmaker. "The ink from the printing was not even dry before he had the fabric in the hands of the dressmaker," Loveless recalled.

It wasn't a matter of artistry alone that caused him to be so conscious of details. Attentive readers of the *Post* diligently inspected his covers for errors. On one cover he had painted a package about to be mailed, and several readers pointed out to him the package was stamped with insufficient postage. After that Rockwell made a point of weighing any similar prop at the post office, to be certain it contained the correct number of stamps.

If Rockwell had any consistent problem in his work it derived from his tendency to overwork a painting, and thereby lose the spontaneity of it by tightening up. This might result in the picture becoming "too photographic" (as he would say himself) or overstated with too *many* details. This temptation on Rockwell's part was cause for differences between him and his wife Mary who continually urged him to finish the painting at a stage before he overworked it or added too many details. Rockwell knew this preoccupation was a weakness, but he found it very difficult to restrain himself. He could become so involved with small details that he might lose sight of some major detail that was wrong or left out. Here he depended on friends to find errors or omissions, such as the time the farmer Jim Edgerton had pointed out that a painting being prepared for a summer cover included a boy wearing a winter hat. No one managed to catch the error in the *Post* cover of the returning soldier: the carpenter at work had no ladder for climbing down from the roof of the porch. Then in another work there was the group of figures with an extra leg. . . .

Rockwell's humor was frequently directed at himself and his worry about details was something he knew had its amusing components. This is probably why he enjoyed painting the April Fool's covers—he did three in all. He could play with details in a way that poked fun at their misuse. "I've fixed the mistake mongers," he laughed after he completed his first such cover in 1944. ("Though of course, I hadn't," he admitted. "I put 45 mistakes and incongruities into the picture; a man wrote me from South America claiming to have found a hundred and twenty.")

Although he envied his friend Mead Schaeffer's speed of execution, Rockwell was unable to paint faster, no matter how he tried. He worked and reworked until he was satisfied, never hesitating to burn a canvas he felt was less than adequate, regardless of the time he had already invested. And his family and friends continued to troop back to the studio to look at the picture.

From time to time the Rockwells would get restless, particularly during a long Vermont winter, and they would be off. Three times during the 1940s they went to live in Mary Rockwell's home state of California. At other times they would visit Cape Cod for a change of pace, or make a quick trip to New York City. Until Mary Rockwell became ill in the early 1950s, the family maintained this consistent pace.

Mary Rockwell's illness required that she make frequent visits to Massachusetts for treatment, and they both decided that it would be more convenient for them to live near the hospital. Norman Rockwell was also ready for the move, still convinced that a new environment every twenty years or so was stimulating. The Rockwells left Arlington to live in Stockbridge, Massachusetts, in 1953, a swiftly-made and executed decision, with no pause for looking back.

OVERLEAF: No painting left the Rockwell studio without the consultation of Rockwell's immediate friends and family. The observations of the cook—Mrs. LaBombard—and her husband were as helpful as those of his wife, his son Peter, and his colleagues. Here the illustrator is consulting his friendly critics about his painting, *Norman Rockwell Visits a Ration Board.*

THE SCHAEFFERS

Mead Schaeffer's illustrations were inspired by the great Brandywine tradition that includes the heroic paintings of Howard Pyle, N.C. Wyeth, and Frank Schoonover. A graduate of Pratt, he began by modeling for Dean Cornwell, and for some time Schaeffer painted in the same studio building as Cornwell and Harvey Dunn, two illustrators working in the Pyle tradition. Like these artists, Schaeffer preferred to illustrate blockbuster stories and novels, regarding magazine covers somehow as the more frivolous aspect of illustration. Schaeffer dreamed of pirates and giants, adventure and romance, heroism and villainy. Frank Dodd of Dodd Mead publishing company was a fishing companion and client, and he commissioned Mead Schaeffer to illustrate nineteen classics over the years, including all the novels by Herman Melville; but book illustration didn't pay as well as magazine work ("not even enough to pay the models," said Schaeffer), so he balanced his efforts with the more lucrative assignments from the periodicals. For a considerable length of time, Schaeffer illustrated two serials a month for such magazines as *Good Housekeeping*, *Cosmopolitan*, and *McCall's*. Each generally required a square and a vignette, with a double-page spread for the opening installment—six pictures in all. "All this called for the expenditure of a tremendous amount of energy, but I was young and enthusiastic," said Schaeffer, "and had acquired a broad, direct manner of working—a technical facility, plus an ability to fake and improvise—which permitted prodigiously rapid accomplishment. Young men are fond of good money, and money came easily, so all in all I was well-satisfied for a long time."

Mead Schaeffer knew Rockwell only casually at the time they both lived in New Rochelle. Their phone conversations consisted primarily of talk of trading models. In particular, they planned their deadlines around the model Fred Hildebrandt.

It was at Hildebrandt's invitation that Schaeffer sampled the marvels of trout fishing on the Batten Kill River. He and his wife Elizabeth took an instant liking to Arlington and bought a house there, settling in the community in 1940, just about the time the Rockwells had decided to live there year round. Situated on the Green River, a tributary of the Batten Kill, the Schaeffers' home was convenient for fishing. "I could fish for my supper. If we wanted to, Fred Hildebrandt, Jack Atherton, and I could fish all night in that beautiful river only steps away from my back door."

Although Rockwell didn't share Schaeffer's zeal for fishing, the two families became virtually inseparable. They would make local car trips together to places like Bennington, or Troy. They traveled to Brandywine territory, Wilmington, Delaware, where they visited N.C. Wyeth, Frank Schoonover, and the Delaware Art Museum, returning with a new spurt of

Mead Schaeffer, shown posing for Rockwell in the photograph on the left, had much in common with his colleague. Their passion for illustration provided an inestimable bond between them. The Schaeffer daughters, Patty and Lee, shown posing with Mary Atherton on the right, were also favorite models for several of the Arlington illustrators, especially Norman Rockwell.

inspiration. They traveled in each other's company for two-and-a-half months in California, and brought back many ideas for illustrations. While artistically they were quite different, Rockwell and Schaeffer admired each other's work, and each encouraged the other in his uniqueness. "In the car Norman and I would be in the front seat, the girls in the back. We'd talk pictures, pictures, pictures, driving from one door to the next, not always agreeing, but always sharing a respect for the other's view. We worked hard and we relaxed easily with each other. It was a marvelous friendship. There's no denying it; that was a period in my life I long for again," Schaeffer reflected wistfully.

As artists, Schaeffer and Rockwell differed in their approach to specificity. Rockwell always looked for a model who was the right "type" to convey the story; Schaeffer was a broad painter, and specific details of individuality and expression were secondary to the overall sweep or mood of the illustration. One model could serve many functions over and over, because facial details were incidental to the movement of the figure. Like other artists inspired by Howard Pyle, Schaeffer worked in a manner that resembles that of the method actor: you *become* the figure as you paint it in an empathetic, almost visceral experience that transcends the recording of the immediate details from behind the easel. Schaeffer worked more comfortably from imagination, from fantasy, inflating reality with a kind of drama and heroism. This approach differed considerably from the thoughtful, carefully constructed and composed details that Rockwell required for his realism.

They benefited from each other by their differences. Rockwell, for example, had a real talent for extracting from a model precisely what was needed for a painting. "Sometimes I'd get a model who was a flat tire," Schaeffer recalled, "and I'd call Norman in to whip him up, to direct him so he'd *feel* the part of the pirate if that was what was needed. Norman was a great ham and knew how to pull that model into his performance."

Elizabeth Schaeffer (nicknamed "Toby") was sixteen years old when she met Mead Schaeffer in school. She had a bright and direct personality and was indispensable to her husband through the years. They would discuss every assignment before he accepted it and share solutions to artistic problems ("she could have taught illustration"). Finally, Elizabeth Schaeffer went to study photography and became quite an expert with the camera, acting as her husband's photographer. She and Mary Rockwell were the supporting elements in the four-way friendship. They frequently made shopping trips together, hunting down props and costumes their husbands needed, and confiding in each other about the difficulties and joys of being married to exalted illustrators. "And we *were* exalted," Schaeffer recalled.

Why, we were going to bring back the Golden Age of Illustration with our enthusiasm. It was more than just an excitement about art—though that was at the heart of it. There was the sense of fellowship and sharing we all felt, a generosity that spurred us onto greater heights. We were there for criticism, to model, to help each other out of a jam. All of us were supportive and eager to see the next guy succeed. That feeling among illustrators just doesn't exist anymore. Neither does the exaltation.

At 5:00—after a good day's work—the Schaeffers and Rockwells and perhaps the Athertons and Hugheses might convene for cocktails, for the "children's hour," as one of them called it. The talk was naturally about pictures, a rapid exchange of ideas that Lee Schaeffer recalls vividly. "Listening to my father and his friends talk about these subjects—and sometimes the conversations became very heated—was inspiring for me as a child. These men were all so committed; so engaged; so purposeful."

Their gatherings at 5:00 were an important form of stimulation in this intimate artists' community. The Schaeffers and Rockwells also entertained the editors and art directors who came through Vermont, people from Hollywood and New York who might come to visit. "Entertaining was an aspect of the business we were in, after all. And four could entertain more easily than two. You could always go to sleep without attracting too much notice."

Norman Rockwell joined his friend on location while Schaef was working on the series of fourteen commemorative war covers for the *Saturday Evening Post*. Rockwell enjoyed meeting the generals and riding in the tanks, though he knew nothing about warfare and never painted combat subjects himself. "He was so boyish. A Will Rogers, if you know what I mean. He had a curiosity and enthusiasm about everything."

The Will Rogers in Rockwell would come out in situations Schaeffer found enviable, such as the time they were invited as distinguished guests to address the Art Directors Club in Chicago at a formal banquet before several hundred professionals. At his turn Rockwell simply rose to the microphone and addressed the group informally as if he'd known everyone

Mead Schaeffer posed for many of his own paintings. (His wife was an accomplished photographer.) By posing himself, Schaeffer was able to "climb into" the subject of his painting, an empathetic approach to painting that was characteristic of this artist.

in the room, typically relaxed and witty. Schaef, on the other hand, was so frightened that he trembled through the entire meal and had a distinctly queasy feeling in his stomach while the others spoke. Although his father had been a minister, Schaef claimed he inherited no oratory skills whatsoever. Standing before the crowd, he grappled for his carefully written-out notes—first in this pocket, then that pocket—without success. He was paralyzed with fear. He lowered his eyes and picked out a friendly, receptive face in the crowd and started to stutter a most unexpected speech: "There are four ways to fish the Batten Kill River," he began, and proceeded to describe the subject most dear to his heart. The topic was unusual for the event at hand, but a great improvement over the treatise on illustration he had prepared so assiduously. Schaef was spared disaster, but he vowed never again to accept such an invitation.

The period of time spent in Arlington greatly influenced Schaeffer's work. He underwent a profound change in direction. He said in a 1945 interview,

> The day had come when I suddenly realized I was sick of it all— sick of painting dudes and dandies, sick of exaggerated sentiment and of artificial romance and love, with the endless succession of 'he and she' pictures. I was tired, too, of the constant struggle to meet deadlines, and of being subject to the moods and caprices of art editors. Especially I was surfeited with the constant faking: my work was supposed to be convincing, but I knew it was not. I longed to do honest work, based on real places, real people, and real things—work expressive of normal human emotions and activities. So I did a right-about-face, and have never regretted it. True, my production lessened, but the satisfaction of doing an honest job in my own way more than compensated.

Like Rockwell, Schaeffer found in Arlington a return to the more fundamental aspects of picture-making. Eventually he left illustration entirely, abandoning his oils, and adopting watercolor instead: an abstractionist, a landscape painter, an honestly creative man who would have painted every day even if he never earned a nickel from doing so.

The Schaeffers left Arlington in 1950 before the Rockwells left. Time and distance separated them over the years. Elizabeth and Mary died. The younger Schaeffer daughter, Patty, met an untimely death. Only the memories of a most unusual friendship remained. "When I went to see Norman in Stockbridge not long before he died, I found him on a bad day. He didn't recognize me at all. Oh, I cried for the past when I left his side. I've never had a friend like him, before or since. I loved the man."

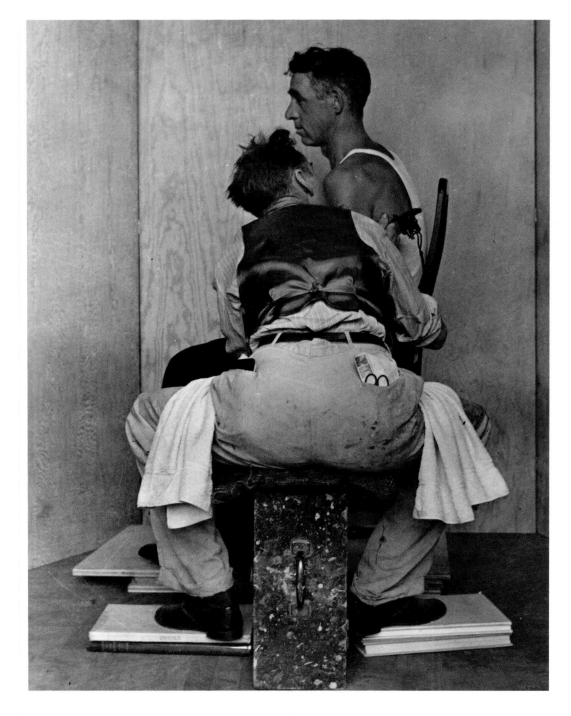

M ead Schaeffer's only appearance as a central figure in a Rockwell illustration was as a tattooist. Despite his objection that Rockwell exaggerated the size of his rump, Schaeffer was delighted to have taken part in a cover that became so popular. To acquire the authentic equipment used in the picture, Rockwell located a tattooist on the Bowery in New York, and consulted with this professional and with former sailors to insure accuracy. The model for the sailor is Clarence Decker, whose daughter Phyllis happened to be the first girl Peter Rockwell ever kissed. Master of the Grange in Arlington, Decker posed for other paintings by Rockwell, including *Strictly a Sharpshooter* and *The Forging Contest.*

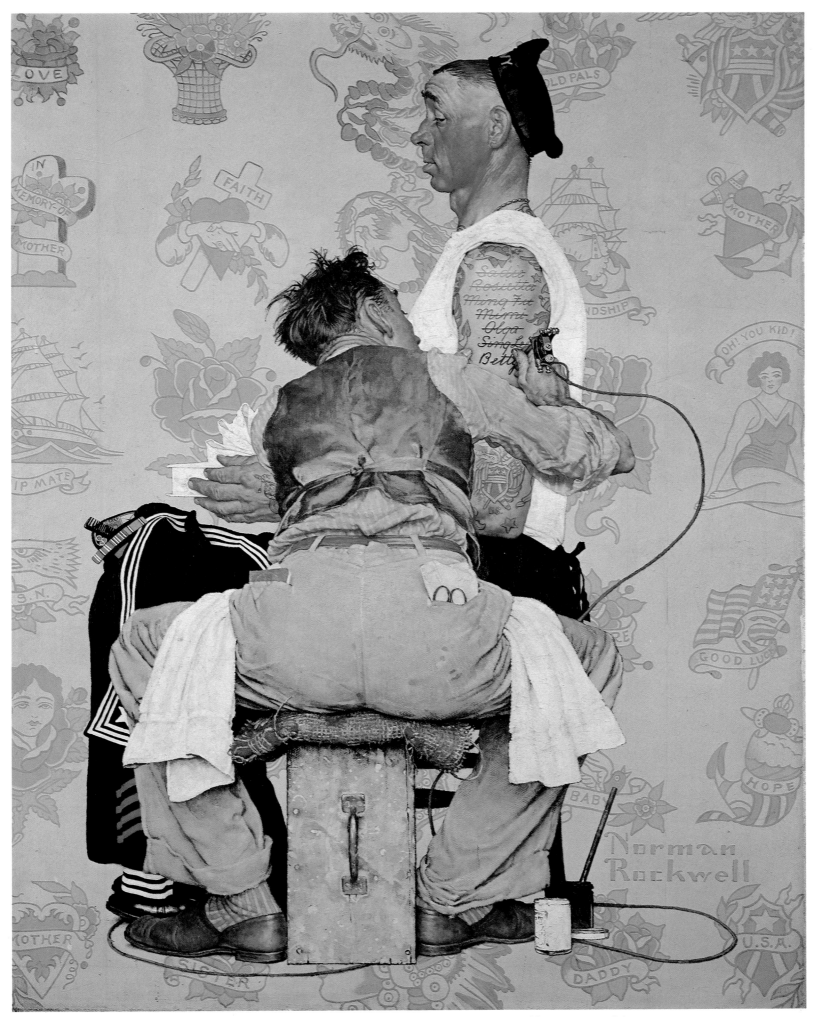

Tattooist. Original oil painting for a *Saturday Evening Post* cover, March 4, 1944. Collection Brooklyn Museum of Art.

Soldiers and Seamen by Mead Schaeffer. Original oil painting for an illustration. Collection Mr. and Mrs. Robert Goodfellow.
Photo Frank Forward.

An Alaskan Story. Original oil painting for an illustration by Mead Schaeffer. Collection the estate of Mead Schaeffer.
Photo Eric Pollitzer.

I n spite of—or perhaps because of—their artistic differ-ences, Norman Rockwell and Mead Schaeffer shared great respect for each other's talents. Unlike Rockwell, Mead Schaeffer used design and color, rather than detail, to convey the story. A single model could be used over and over in Schaeffer's illustrations because the artist focused on broad shapes and movement, gener-alizing matters of specifics, and painting rapidly to capture the overall composition and mood. Schaeffer's debt to Howard Pyle and Dean Cornwell are evident in his daring and romantic approach to his subject. "Schaef is a slight, agile man," said Rockwell. "Yet he has tremendous ability for painting the powerful, broad-shouldered, heroic man, sheer physical courage, man against nature. . . . His illustrations give one a real sense of robust, swashbuckling manhood. His attitude toward life is the same as that in his paintings."

Embracing Man and Woman by Mead Schaeffer. Original oil painting for an illustration. Collection Mr. and Mrs. Robert Goodfellow.
Photo Frank Forward.

The Point of File by Mead Schaeffer. Original oil painting for a *Saturday Evening Post* cover, October 24, 1942. Courtesy Judy and Alan Goffman Fine Art, Blue Bell, Pennsylvania.

The Tank Commander by Mead Schaeffer. Original oil painting for a *Saturday Evening Post* cover, January 9, 1943. Courtesy Judy and Alan Goffman Fine Art, Blue Bell, Pennsylvania.

The Engineer Corps by Mead Schaeffer. Original oil painting for a *Saturday Evening Post* cover, October 28, 1944. Courtesy Judy and Alan Goffman Fine Art, Blue Bell, Pennsylvania.

The Heavy Artillery by Mead Schaeffer. Original oil painting for a *Saturday Evening Post* cover, November 6, 1943. Courtesy Judy and Alan Goffman Fine Art, Blue Bell, Pennsylvania.

Carrier Signal Lieutenant by Mead Schaeffer. Original oil painting for a *Saturday Evening Post* cover, June 12, 1943. Courtesy Judy and Alan Goffman Fine Art, Blue Bell, Pennsylvania.

Norman Rockwell and Mead Schaeffer were both eager to make a real contribution to the war effort. Sketches in hand, they ventured to Washington, D.C., to volunteer their illustrations to the War Office. Their generous offer was declined. On their way back from Washington they stopped off at Philadelphia to see Ben Hibbs at the *Post*. Hibbs immediately invited Rockwell and Schaeffer to apply their talents to wartime subjects, knowing the inspirational value of such paintings in a time of national crisis. Rockwell painted his *Four Freedoms* for the *Post*, and Schaeffer completed a total of fourteen covers honoring the American forces in com-

bat. This series necessitated several trips to military facilities, and whenever time permitted, Rockwell joined Schaeffer. Although Rockwell painted only one combat picture himself (a war poster), he enjoyed these excursions with Schaeffer to the bases—bumping along on a dusty road in a jeep and examining the tanks. Like their other trips together, these were filled with an intense exchange of ideas and humor. "This friendship with Schaef," Rockwell said, "a working illustrator, someone who shared my ideals, understood my problems—stimulated me. I guess it helped my work almost as much as moving to Arlington."

Strictly a Sharpshooter. Original oil painting for story of same title by D.D. Beauchamp, *American Magazine*, June, 1941. Old Corner House Collection, Stockbridge, Massachusetts.

Of all the models Rockwell used here only the fighter at the left was authentic. The others represented imaginative portrayals of Rockwell's friends and neighbors. He selected Elizabeth Schaeffer for the female in the painting, a role that was certainly out of character. "She is really a fine lady," Rockwell asserted. Other models doubled up: Rockwell's Arlington photographer and assistant Gene Pelham appears in the crowd as the man with a cigar and in the ring ministering to the boxer at the left. Nip Noyes, the East Arlington postman, appears twice also, wearing a bowler derby in both instances. The twisted expression on the boxer who is standing above Elizabeth Schaeffer was produced for Rockwell by Clarence Decker, the sailor in *The Tattooist*. The setting and subject were so unfamiliar to Rockwell, in fact, that he spent a considerable amount of time at a boxing club on Manhattan's Columbus Circle to study the types likely to frequent such an establishment. 🍎

Fixing a Flat. *Saturday Evening Post* cover, August 3, 1946.

The Convention. Saturday Evening Post cover, May 3, 1941.

The Schaeffers had two daughters—Lee and Patty— who posed several times for Rockwell. They were a peppy pair and Rockwell used them when he wanted a lively teenager or a saucy blonde. The two sisters were painted together for *Fixing a Flat.* "He told me that he was incapable of painting a sexy girl," Peter Rockwell related when talking about his father's rendition of Lee Schaeffer as the blonde in the convertible. "They always came out looking funny, rather than sexy." This "failing" on Rockwell's part (actually, he was proud of it), did not prevent him from depicting a very appealing female in two of the paintings for the Willie Gillis series. "I fell in love with Willie Gillis's girl when I saw her on the cover of the *Saturday Evening Post*," boasted Bob Goodfellow, Lee Schaeffer's husband. 🍎

The Flirts. Original oil painting for a *Saturday Evening Post* cover, July 26, 1941. Harry N. Abrams Family Collection.

New Year's Eve Without Willie Gillis. *Saturday Evening Post* cover, January 1, 1944.

Arguing Over Willie Gillis. *Saturday Evening Post* cover, September 5, 1942.

THE ATHERTONS

John Atherton had great affection for his friends Mead Schaeffer and Norman Rockwell, but he did not share their passion for illustration. He was an illustrator himself, of course, but only out of necessity. Commercial work simply financed his two other passions: fishing and easel painting. And he was a master of both.

Like Mead Schaeffer, Jack Atherton was drawn to Arlington for its excellent fishing. Meeting at the Society of Illustrators one evening in 1941, Norman Rockwell invited Atherton to sample the trout on the Batten Kill. After a brief visit, Maxine and John Atherton decided to leave Ridgefield, Connecticut, and settle permanently in Arlington.

The Athertons had originally come East from San Francisco, where they had met in art school. The prosperous community of Ridgefield, where they lived for several years, was convenient to New York City, but they found it difficult to maintain two very different groups of friends. Having been an outdoorsman all his life, Jack Atherton was in frequent demand for hunting, fishing, and golf. An excellent shot, he participated in a number of very fashionable field trials. He was equally intimate with another, very different sector of the community. Because his mother was a professional pianist, and he had worked his way through art school playing the banjo in a jazz band, Atherton had a keen appreciation for music as well, and was drawn to the company of other musicians. The two groups did not intermingle comfortably, however. "My father explained what was meant by the 'Restricted' sign posted at the entrance of the Ridgefield Country Club (of which he was not a member). It seemed astonishing that the musicians we loved and admired could not be admitted because they were Jews."

In Arlington, Jack Atherton was more successful in blending the many components of his life. The *Saturday Evening Post* paid him sufficiently well to permit him the time and energy for easel painting. Maxine and Jack Atherton, both avid fishermen, found the northern streams and rivers easily accessible and productive. They built a house right on the Batten Kill, the most contemporary home in Arlington, which was referred to as "the chicken house" by the more traditional neighbors. Intellectual stimulation was plentiful: they quickly found musicians, writers, and artists living nearby, and each week they drove to Bennington for concerts at the college.

In temperament Atherton was very different from Rockwell. A man of firm convictions, he was easily annoyed by the things he disliked. Rockwell said, "Whenever something irritated him—and something did almost every day, for his threshold of irritability was low—he'd groan and wrap his arms around his head and sway from side to side as if you were sticking red-hot knives in him." He disliked doing illustrations for ads—despised their silly restrictions—and he was annoyed by any form of sentimentality in art, avoiding human interest pictures whenever he could. He preferred painting

Ready for Action by John Atherton. Painting for a *Saturday Evening Post* cover, December 12, 1942.

Spirit of Kansas City. Painted in collaboration with Jack Atherton. Undated.

coolly surreal still-lifes and landscapes, later turning to abstraction.

In spite of their differences, Rockwell and Atherton were loyal friends, each in great admiration of the other's talents. Rockwell particularly respected Atherton's facility as an artist.

> Jack Atherton was capable of separating his commercial work from his fine arts work and looking on each with a different viewpoint. He could do an abstraction in the morning, painting only to satisfy himself, brooking no interference from others.... And in the afternoon he could start a *Post* cover, making sure that it had the correct proportions and that the idea was clear and absolutely comprehensive to everyone.... I guess one of the reasons that Jack was able to do both commercial and fine arts work was his extraordinary facility. He could use any medium, letter beautifully. And he always knew just what he was going to do each time he put brush to canvas, pencil to paper.... Everything Jack did— skiing, tennis, painting, fishing, skating—he did to perfection. Something inside him forced him to excel, though it wasn't particularly competitive. It was more, I always thought, a deep abhorrence of sloppiness, of amateurishness, of slip-shod performance in anything.

For his part, Atherton returned this esteem equally. He never understood why Rockwell accepted so many commercial assignments (the Boy Scout calendars he referred to as "propaganda, sentimental trash"), but he defended Rockwell's work when anyone else criticized it, and promoted his friend to others when there was an opportunity to do so. In an effort to arouse more serious critical interest in Rockwell's work, Atherton invited Robert Coates, an art writer for *The New Yorker*, to Rockwell's studio and was disgusted with the critic's neutral response.

Rockwell and Atherton occasionally worked together. Atherton created a pattern for Rockwell to use as a wallpaper design in his *Post* cover, *Facts of Life*, and they both collaborated on a poster for Kansas City called *The Spirit of Kansas City* (Rockwell painted the figure; Atherton the background), an unlikely collaboration that produced a work bearing little resemblance to that of either artist.

The *Post* illustrators were frequently in each other's company, meeting for cocktails and dinner throughout the year when time permitted. Each Thanksgiving and Christmas—if they happened to be in town at the same time—the Athertons and Schaeffers came together for a feast at the Rockwells'. "Shop talk and art talk" is what Maxine Atherton remembered about those convivial gatherings. "And always a lot of laughter." Atherton had a fine sense of humor, except when it came to subjects he took very seriously. He willingly posed for Rockwell's April Fool's cover—submitting to being portrayed as a fisherman who does everything wrong—but he

Unlike Norman Rockwell and Mead Schaeffer, John Atherton was more intense about fine art than he was about illustration, and he tended to favor landscape and still life to the human figure. Even when he collaborated with Norman Rockwell for *The Spirit of Kansas City*, Rockwell painted the figure (Walt Squires) and John Atherton did the background. Both signed the painting. As a result of his preference, Atherton's magazine covers tended to tell their stories through symbols rather than action. He particularly enjoyed assignments that permitted him to draw on his love for outdoor sports, such as the *Post* cover shown opposite.

would not accept the painting when Rockwell offered it as a gift. Fishing was just too sacred for such tomfoolery.

If they had a choice, the Athertons would have stayed in Arlington forever. Life was very good to them there. Their daughter Mary was in college at Bennington; they had a stimulating group of friends; and they took many fishing trips. Atherton had been invited to lecture; he judged art competitions, and even found time to write and illustrate a book on his favorite subject called *Fly and the Fish.* An increasing number of collectors was taking interest in his fine art, and he was preparing for a one-man show at the Famous Artists Schools in Connecticut. All this came to an end suddenly when, on a fishing trip on the Salmon River in Canada, Jack Atherton died of a heart attack. It was 1952. Maxine Atherton drove back to Arlington, escorted by George Hughes, and stayed with the Rockwells until she felt able to put her home in order. Almost immediately afterward she and her daughter moved to New York. Arlington was not the same without Jack Atherton. "I doubt if I will ever meet a man as volatile and stimulating, or have a friend as loyal," Rockwell said.

John Atherton's work was executed carefully, with close attention to a linear design treatment, quite opposite to Schaeffer's painterly dabs of thick color. It is not surprising that over the years Atherton's work evolved to pure abstraction. A highly respected fine artist, Atherton had his paintings handled by a distinguished New York gallery, and was widely collected by museums. "Jack wasn't set on reviving the golden age of illustration as Schaef and I were," recalled Rockwell, "but he joined in our discussions of art, damning sentimental, human-interest pictures one minute, the next loyally (and violently) upbraiding us for down-grading our work, which was, after all, human interest and (some of it anyway) sentimental."

Original oil painting by John Atherton. Collection Chris and Mary Schafer.
Photo Frank Forward.

Oil painting by John Atherton for *House and Garden*, June, 1930. Copyright © 1930 (renewed) by the Condé Nast Publications, Inc. Courtesy Murray Tinkelman.

Rockwell never really comprehended the passion Mead Schaeffer and Jack Atherton shared for fishing. He particularly didn't understand the purpose of fishing all day without enjoying the benefits of the catch at dinner. Instead, Schaeffer and Atherton would toss the fish back into the river as soon as they hooked it, starting the process all over again. This bewildering activity provided an ideal subject for Rockwell to satirize in an April Fool's cover for the *Post*. Atherton agreed to pose for the picture, but out of respect for the sport could not bring himself to accept the original painting as a gift when Rockwell offered it. Although Rockwell may have been unfair to the sport, he managed to achieve a fair likeness of his friend whom he described this way: "Jack was a large, hulking man with powerful shoulders and big hands and arms. But his head was curiously small, and round and completely bald except for a fringe of light brown hair about his ears."

April Fool. Saturday Evening Post cover, March 31, 1945.

THE HUGHESES

Until World War II, George Hughes had been known for his fashion drawings and his story illustrations—maritime adventure and romance. When the *Post* invited Hughes to do covers after the war, his anticipation of steady work enabled him to live away from the city. Recently married for the second time, he and his wife Casey chose Arlington because it was close to skiing, had a rural atmosphere, and because he would be able to utilize some of the same models the other *Post* illustrators were already using. Of these artists Hughes knew only Jack Atherton.

George and Casey Hughes bought a farm in 1946 and immediately threw a party to become acquainted with their Arlington neighbors. The other artists were delighted to accept the invitation, and Norman Rockwell suggested that it would be especially amusing if Hughes put on a costume party in his newly acquired home. The Hugheses thought this was a fine idea, and Rockwell came dressed in an elaborate eighteenth-century military uniform. "He loved costume parties," said Hughes, recalling another occasion when Rockwell asked him to come to a costume party staged on the theme of the World War I armistice. Rockwell suggested they go as Zouaves, Algerian soldiers in the French Army. The two of them rented splendid outfits from a theatrical costume supplier in New York City—

As an illustrator, George Hughes came from a very different orientation from that of his colleagues Norman Rockwell, Mead Schaeffer, and Jack Atherton. Fashion was his forte, an appreciation for high style and modern life. Younger than the others, Hughes's work influenced a younger generation of illustrators. Many commercial artists of the 1950s looked toward his crisp color and audacious composition for inspiration. Drawing from the same Arlington models his friends were using, Hughes entirely transformed these familiar faces and figures. Lee and Patty Schaeffer—Mead Schaeffer's daughters, who fixed the flat in Rockwell's illustration—were portrayed by Hughes as two working girls in a city bus, exclaiming over a diamond engagement ring. Buddy Edgerton—Rockwell's favorite Boy Scout—was converted by Hughes into a lean young man whose romance on a Long Island beach has been interrupted. These differences made the Arlington art community of four seem far greater in scale.

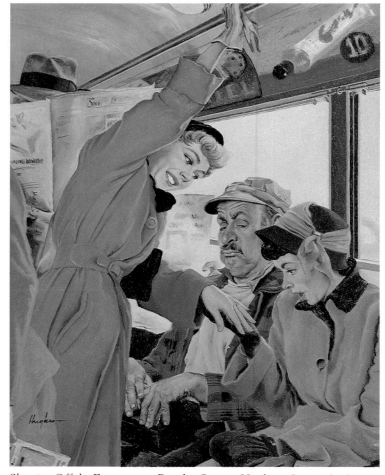

Showing Off the Engagement Ring by George Hughes. Original oil painting for a *Saturday Evening Post* cover, January 22, 1949. Courtesy Judy and Alan Goffman Fine Art, Blue Bell, Pennsylvania.

The Night Before Christmas by George Hughes. Original oil painting for a *Saturday Evening Post* cover, December 24, 1949. Courtesy Judy and Alan Goffman Fine Art, Blue Bell, Pennsylvania.

Writing Christmas Thank Yous by George Hughes. Original oil painting for a *Saturday Evening Post* cover, January 9, 1960. Courtesy Judy and Alan Goffman Fine Art, Blue Bell, Pennsylvania.

Summer Romance Spoiled by George Hughes. Original oil painting for a *Saturday Evening Post* cover, August 6, 1954. Courtesy Judy and Alan Goffman Fine Art, Blue Bell, Pennsylvania.

Rockwell was well known there for other rentals—and arrived made up and outfitted as an identical pair.

It wasn't long before the Hugheses were at home in Arlington. Two years after they arrived in Vermont they decided to abandon any notion of farming and sold their house to Chris and Mary Schafer, moving to another home nearby. As Hughes had anticipated, Arlington's models suited his purposes. He painted Buddy Edgerton, Elizabeth and Lee Schaeffer, Mary Whalen, Chris and Mary Schafer and their children. Unlike Rockwell, Hughes was not very drawn to what he called "the all-American type," preferring instead a more cosmopolitan personality. Having illustrated for automobile advertisements, for *Vanity Fair* and *House and Garden*, Hughes felt greater kinship with the sophisticated tastes and situations of the upper-middle class, and he tended to paint more urban themes. While Rockwell sought out authentic rural characters for his illustrations, Hughes would dress up his models to play the cosmopolitan roles he constructed for them. Buddy Edgerton became an East Hampton beach boy; the Schafers' daughter Christina became a debutante; Chris and Mary Schafer became a romantic duo.

In fact, Hughes suspected that Rockwell solicited his advice on paintings in order to determine what *not* to do with a picture in progress. Rockwell asked Hughes into the studio to give him a reaction to his current project,

Waiting for the Art Editor. Old Corner House Collection, Stockbridge, Massachusetts.

Outside the Principal's Office. "What do you think of it?" Rockwell asked, turning the canvas toward Hughes. "I think it's fine," the latter responded. "*Now* what do you think of it?" Rockwell asked, laying an overlay onto the canvas that introduced another figure into the scene. "I prefer the first version," Hughes said. Rockwell turned to his wife who was standing nearby, "You see, Mary, he prefers the first version!" as if there had been a dispute between them over the two possibilities. Hughes felt quite satisfied with the exchange, until the *Post* cover appeared several weeks later, Rockwell having decided on the second version, after all. "I think he calculated that if I liked a painting it was too high-toned, so he did just the opposite."

Hughes remembered another incident when he talked about a painting with Rockwell at Jack Atherton's house one winter evening. "I've been working on this painting all week and it's going nowhere," lamented Rockwell. "Today I got so mad at it that I threw it out of the studio, right into the snow. I think maybe the idea stinks." Hughes inquired about the nature of the subject, and Rockwell described it: "It's an old lady sitting in a railroad diner with a kid and they're praying at the table. A bunch of toughs are looking over at them."

"You're right," Hughes declared. "The idea stinks."

Hughes is now convinced that his response (truthfully expressed) was all Rockwell needed to have himself retrieve the painting from the snow the next day and return to work on it. Hughes also acknowledges that this painting, *Saying Grace*, is among Rockwell's finest achievements. "Norman always ended up doing what he wanted to do anyway, no matter how much advice he asked. That's why he was so good."

Hughes's feelings for Rockwell went far deeper than simple professional admiration. He was frequently struck by Rockwell's thoughtfulness, such as the time his daughter by his first marriage was getting married. Hughes was preparing for the trip to New York to give her away at the wedding when Rockwell phoned. "Norman felt that my going to the wedding might be somewhat of an ordeal for me—especially since I would be seeing so many old friends from my first marriage. On the phone he announced that he was coming with me to the wedding to keep me company. Then Chris Schafer said he wanted to come, too. Their presence made it easier for me, but I never would have asked. It was like Norman to offer without being asked."

George Hughes posed for Norman Rockwell only once, but the *Post* cover illustration never developed beyond the drawing stage. The idea came to Rockwell when he and Hughes were both calling on the *Post* headquarters in Philadelphia. Rockwell was excited about recreating the publication's waiting room, and had the brilliant leather chairs shipped to his Arlington studio. Hughes was depicted as the urbane figure at the right.

THE ART STUDENTS

Although Rockwell was always happy to *talk* about painting, he took little interest in *teaching* the subject. In 1950 he made an exception by taking on a few students for the summer. Rockwell—fearing he was growing rusty in his work and ideas—felt that some younger illustrators might prove stimulating and might be an encouraging group to have near his gifted son Jarvis who was also painting at the time.

He notified the Art Students League of his intention and suggested the faculty invite their best students on his behalf. William McNulty approached his student Don Spaulding with this unique invitation, and the twenty-four year old student jumped at the chance to study with the great illustrator. Although Spaulding was personally attracted to the subjects and techniques of another contemporary illustrator—the eminent Western artist Harold von Schmidt—Spaulding was thrilled with the prospect of working with Rockwell. He never regretted his decision. By the end of the five months in Arlington, Spaulding changed his approach entirely and never returned to his former methods.

Four other students came from the League with Spaulding—Don Winslow, Robert Hogue, Jim Gaboda, and Harold Stevenson. William McBride, Rockwell's own choice, also joined the group.

The six art students lived and worked in the schoolhouse on the West Arlington Green, the place that Rockwell had used six years before as a temporary studio until the carpenter Walt Squires had completed construction on the new studio behind the house. On a platform at the back of the room that had once served as the stage for the schoolhouse, the kitchen and dormitory living quarters were set up. Several paintings by Rockwell and two original Mead Schaeffers hung on the walls.

The method of instruction was casual. Rockwell gave them informal assignments and arranged for models to pose. He might saunter in during the day to comment on their work, or the students would join Rockwell in his studio later for a critique. Rockwell invited Mead Schaeffer, Jack Atherton, and George Hughes to talk with them. It was a fine experience for a serious student of illustration like Don Spaulding, an opportunity to witness the practical application of what he had been learning in art school.

Most inspiring for Don Spaulding was watching Rockwell at work. Rockwell shared with them all stages of the painting in progress—planning, photography, painting—the methodical techniques unraveled before their eyes. "Watching him paint was like being reborn. It looked so easy. I'd think, 'If I just apply myself I can do that, too.' I couldn't wait to get back to the easel, but the next time I'd work, I couldn't accomplish what he did, no matter how much I applied myself. He simply came onto this earth a genius." On the other hand, Spaulding learned from Rockwell the value of

The one-room schoolhouse on the West Arlington green served admirably as an art studio. During the summer of 1950, six art students came to study with Norman Rockwell. They lived and worked in the old schoolhouse. Don Spaulding and Don Winslow—two of the six students—are studying the paintings by Rockwell and Schaeffer that were hung on the walls for inspiration.

OVERLEAF: The interior and exterior of the schoolhouse are shown on the next page. Also shown is the photograph taken by Don Spaulding during a hike that summer. Here Norman Rockwell is standing with Peter Rockwell, Robert Hogue, and Don Winslow.

Photos courtesy Don Spaulding.

discipline and hard work, knowing that even this genius struggled with such problems as perspective. At times Rockwell simplified the technique, using a one-point perspective, perhaps, but at other times confronted his limitations, resolving them with determination in more complex treatments, such as in *Shuffleton's Barber Shop*. "He never took the easy way out. He never faked anything." For students who could become discouraged easily, witnessing this determination was gratifying. Equally inspiring to them was Rockwell's enthusiasm for the painting process. His newest illustration challenged him, and he happily shared his excitement in a boyish drive to explore new territories with each painting.

The group of students left Arlington after the summer, but Don Spaulding stayed into late fall, and Don Winslow continued to live in the schoolhouse for several more years. Winslow acted as Rockwell's apprentice for a while, tracing the drawings onto the canvas, or painting in an occasional background that required tedious application. (For a version of *Facts of Life*, Winslow painted a wallpapered background whose pattern had been designed by Jack Atherton.) Rockwell did his best to encourage this younger artist. He introduced Winslow to an agent and gave him help with his work when a painting wasn't going quite right. But Winslow wasn't fortunate enough to have Rockwell's even disposition. His temperament was not well suited to the demanding deadlines imposed by unsympathetic clients and his moods would rise and fall unpredictably.

Don Spaulding bought a summer home near Arlington and returned frequently to see his friends. Commissioned to do covers for Lone Ranger and Buck Jones comic books, Spaulding would take advantage of these visits by photographing the Arlington neighbors in the schoolhouse: Carl Hess, Alvie Robertson, and Buddy Edgerton.

The Art Students • 99

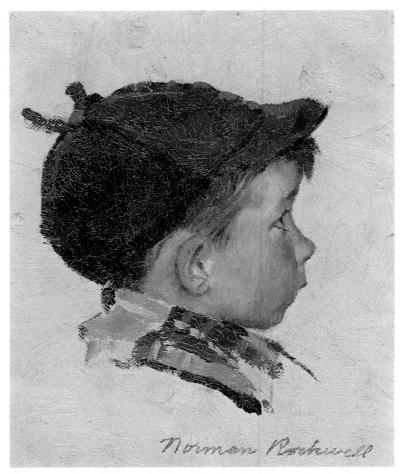

Demonstration oil sketch for Don Winslow by Norman Rockwell.
Courtesy Don Spauding.

Although a talented illustrator, Don Winslow was afflicted with unexpected bouts of depression that tended to interfere with his production. Making every attempt to encourage the young man, Rockwell hired him as an apprentice and introduced him to an agent in New York City. Rockwell would also help with technical problems, such as the time when Winslow became frustrated with his inability to render the head of a young boy in one of his paintings. Rockwell made a rapid oil sketch for him to demonstrate the approach to the task and by copying Rockwell's sketch, Winslow was able to complete the assignment.

During the years Don Winslow lived in the one-room schoolhouse, Rockwell asked him to model several times. Winslow posed for *Saying Grace* among others. Placing Don Winslow and Gene Pelham in front of Mary Rockwell's dressing table, the illustrator achieved what he wanted for *Plumbers in a Boudoir.* 🐝

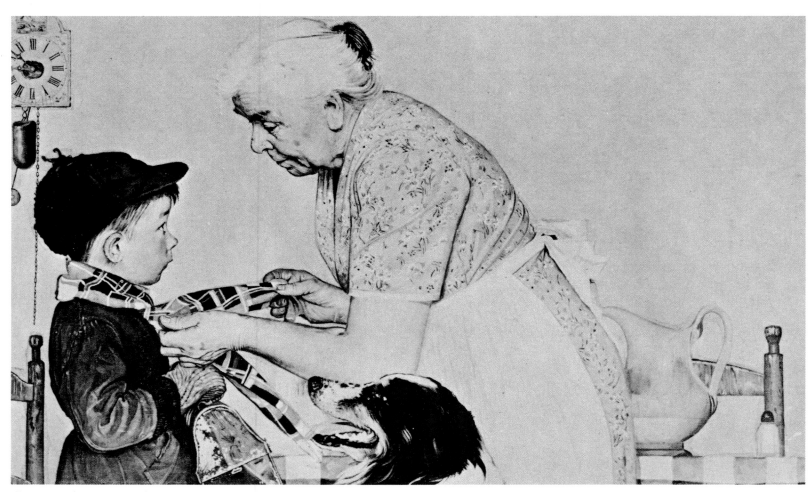

Illustration by Don Winslow.

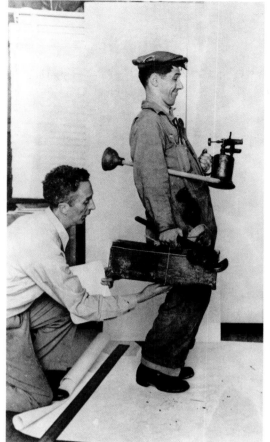

Plumbers in a Boudoir. Original oil painting for a *Saturday Evening Post* cover, June 2, 1951. Collection Gordon Andrew.

Four comic book covers by Don Spaulding. Courtesy Don Spaulding.

Buddy Edgerton.

Carl Hess.

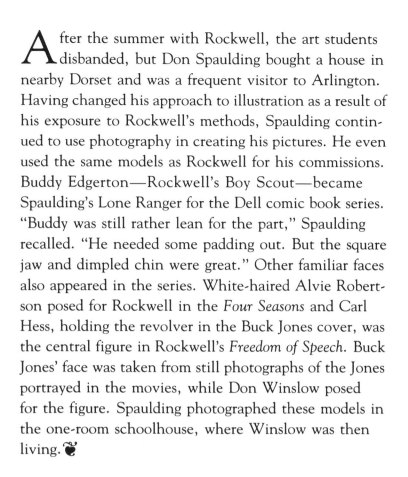

After the summer with Rockwell, the art students disbanded, but Don Spaulding bought a house in nearby Dorset and was a frequent visitor to Arlington. Having changed his approach to illustration as a result of his exposure to Rockwell's methods, Spaulding continued to use photography in creating his pictures. He even used the same models as Rockwell for his commissions. Buddy Edgerton—Rockwell's Boy Scout—became Spaulding's Lone Ranger for the Dell comic book series. "Buddy was still rather lean for the part," Spaulding recalled. "He needed some padding out. But the square jaw and dimpled chin were great." Other familiar faces also appeared in the series. White-haired Alvie Robertson posed for Rockwell in the *Four Seasons* and Carl Hess, holding the revolver in the Buck Jones cover, was the central figure in Rockwell's *Freedom of Speech*. Buck Jones' face was taken from still photographs of the Jones portrayed in the movies, while Don Winslow posed for the figure. Spaulding photographed these models in the one-room schoolhouse, where Winslow was then living. 🍏

Don Winslow.

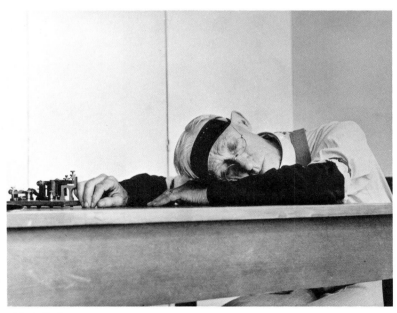

Alvie Robertson.

THE EDGERTONS

When Rockwell's studio burned to the ground one night in 1943, Norman and Mary Rockwell decided not to rebuild the structure but to move somewhere less isolated instead. The day after reaching this decision, they bought a house on the village green in West Arlington, which was yet another example of a Rockwell decision swiftly made and executed.

The house they selected was one of two overlooking the green, the twin structures separated by a mere fifty feet. Only good neighbors could have lived so close by. "If anyone but Jim and Clara Edgerton had lived in the house beside the one for sale, I don't think I would have bought it," commented Rockwell. "But Jim and Clara are about the nicest and finest people I've ever known. I didn't worry about living so close to them, I positively jumped at the chance."

Unlike their new neighbors, the Edgertons were native Vermonters. Jim Edgerton's mother—who lived with them until she went into a nursing home—was only nine months old in 1876 when the family bought the house, and nearly all the Edgerton children were born in the bedroom upstairs. In spite of their different backgrounds, Rockwell had a deep appreciation of both the hardships and benefits derived from the small dairy farm that barely managed to support the Edgertons and their four children. "Farming is a hard life in Vermont," Rockwell explained. "The growing season is short; there's little flat land; the fields are rocky. Jim has had especially hard luck. One year he lost his herd through disease; another year he lost it when the barn floor caved in and choked the cows in their stanchions. But the hard life and misfortune haven't soured Jim and Clara. I don't think they know how to be mean-spirited or nasty."

"We were poor, maybe," said Buddy Edgerton, "but we were rich in so many ways." No one in the family—not Clara, Jim, Edith, Joy, Buddy, or Ardis—felt strange about having the famous illustrator so close. "He was just one of us," they agreed, "and so were Mary and the kids."

The Edgertons particularly recall spending Christmas Day with the Rockwells each year. While their turkey was cooking in the oven, the children would dash over to the Rockwells' house to discover what was left for them under the tree. Brown & Bigelow, the company for which Rockwell illustrated calendars, always sent a large box of almond crunch candy as well as other surprises the Edgerton kids found special. While they opened their presents, and admired the more elaborate Rockwell gifts, Mrs. Rockwell (Norman's mother) sat in a rocker nearby, skinning a large portion of almonds for the Christmas meal. A Norman Rockwell scene, to be sure.

Buddy Edgerton was an extremely handsome young man and his athletic figure, dimpled chin, and square jaw provided an ideal Boy Scout for Rockwell, a Lone Ranger for Don Spaulding, a romantic youth for George Hughes's pictures. From the time he was fourteen until he outgrew the part and was replaced by Freeman Grout, Buddy Edgerton was Rockwell's favorite Boy Scout. Buddy needed to join no formal troop to indulge in Boy Scout activities. He hunted and fished (often with Tom Rockwell) and generally bought fishhooks with the money earned from modeling. Years later the illustrator requested the Edgerton services once again and this time both Buddy and his son Jimmy were used to illustrate the evolution from Cub Scout to Scout Master.

Jim Edgerton was known for his gentle disposition and generosity, a man very much loved by anyone who knew him. He could always be counted on to sign for a loan, even if he didn't have much money, or to help with haying a field when a neighbor was short-handed. He was less likely to impose on others when he needed help. Except with Norman Rockwell. There were times, Buddy Edgerton recalls, when his father made a purchase at a cattle or equipment auction but didn't have the cash to cover expenses. In a simple but revealing measure of the trust each had for the other, Jim Edgerton felt free to borrow the money from Rockwell until the milk checks arrived, when he'd return the sum to his friend. "My father was a very proud man," said Buddy Edgerton, "too proud to have borrowed from anyone else."

While the Rockwells' friendship with the Schaeffers, Athertons, Hugheses, and Schafers tended to be somewhat social, the Edgertons were more like family. Ardis was a baby-sitter to Peter; Joy helped Mary with kitchen work. For the painting of Mrs. O'Leary's cow (which was never published), Buddy Edgerton rounded up his prize-winning 4-H cow and modeled it for Rockwell. Clara ran errands for the Rockwells, frequently catching a train to New York or Philadelphia to deliver a finished painting, or driving Mary to Stockbridge for treatments when needed.

The Rockwells left Arlington in 1953. Jim Edgerton gave up farming in the 1960s, the children married, and Jim passed away in 1979, only months after Norman Rockwell died in Stockbridge. "When I finally moved away from Arlington," Rockwell said, "the thing I most regretted was leaving Jim and Clara."

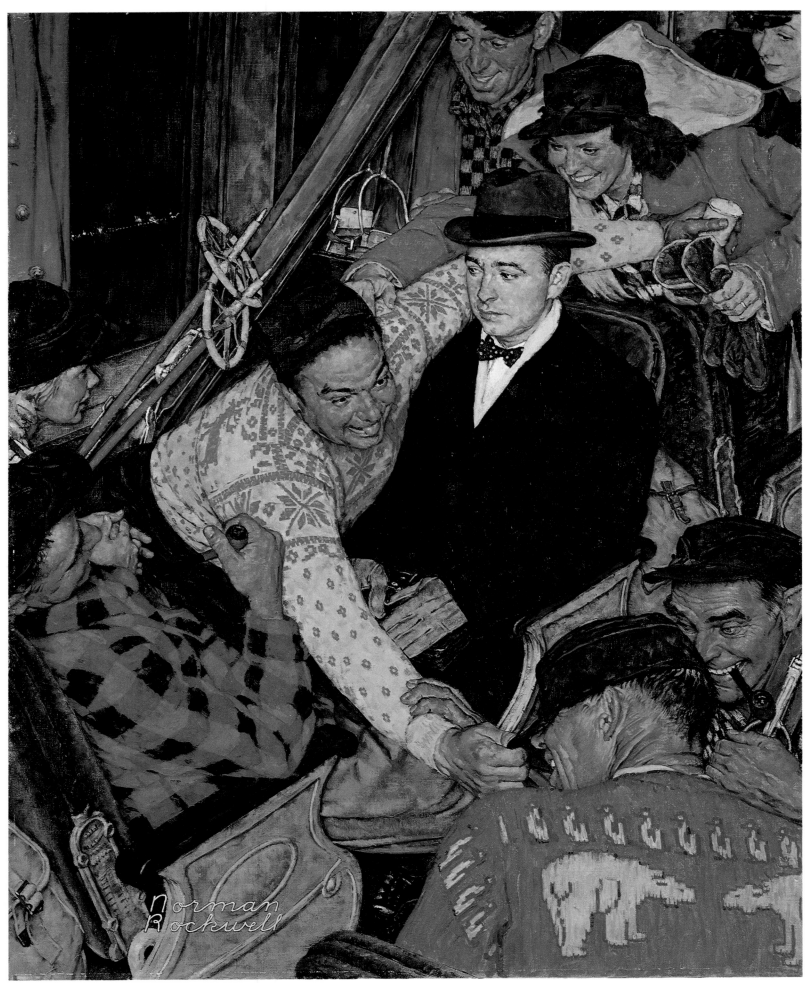

Ski Train. Original oil painting for a *Saturday Evening Post* cover, January 24, 1948.

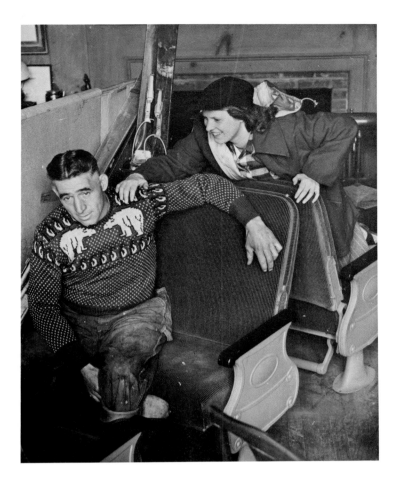

Willie Gillis with Food Package. Saturday Evening Post cover, October 4, 1941.

Living immediately next door to the Rockwells, the Edgerton family was in constant contact with the illustrator. Rockwell could turn to the Edgertons if he needed a painting delivered, a baby-sitter, or a model. Jim Edgerton posed for the first of the famous Willie Gillis series (*Post*, October 4, 1941). His face, cleverly disguised with different facial expressions and cap positions, appears in three of the six heads marching behind Willie. (Gene Pelham is the figure on the right.) Clara Edgerton maintains that this was the last picture Rockwell painted from life.

For *Ski Train* (*Post*, January 24, 1948), Clara Edgerton also doubled as model for two figures, posing for the blonde woman at the left and the brunette in the red jacket at the right. (Gene Pelham appears here as well, the prankster in the center.) For this painting Rockwell had the coach seats shipped from Albany to his Arlington studio. For his earlier train scene (*Post*, August 12, 1944), Rockwell was even more ambitious: he asked the Rutland Railroad to leave a car side-tracked in Rutland, Vermont for him. ("People would do anything for Norman," Don Spaulding had said.) During two very cold days in the winter of 1943, Rockwell posed his models and photographed them inside the unheated coach car. Clara Edgerton's part here was small: the brush of blonde hair in the lower left corner. Others appearing in this painting include Roy Crofut as the soldier and Yvonne Cross as the girl seated alongside her mother, Gladys Cross. The hand of the train conductor at the right belongs to Gene Pelham.

Mrs. O'Leary's Cow. Courtesy Martin Diamond Fine Arts, New York.

Buddy—the only Edgerton son—was a favorite Arlington model. Athletic and handsome, Buddy Edgerton was a splendid Boy Scout, Lone Ranger, or romantic lead. Rockwell used him frequently, not simply because of his good looks, but also because of his gentle and reliable disposition. For example, Rockwell knew he could count on Buddy Edgerton to negotiate the cumbersome task of photographing Mrs. O'Leary's cow for a Brown & Bigelow calendar. With Buddy's prize 4-H project—a docile heifer—in place, Rockwell set up his photography session in the Edgerton's cow barn. The key parts of Bossie were photographed individually, Buddy nudging her head to face the camera, the hindquarters snapped from a safe distance—and the boy received the standard $5.00 fee for the session. The completed painting (with the Rockwells' cook, Elizabeth LaBombard, posed as Mrs. O'Leary) was eventually rejected. "The publisher suspected that no one would want to look at the rear end of a cow hanging on the wall for a full calendar year," recalled Buddy Edgerton.

Every year Norman Rockwell painted an official Boy Scout calendar for Brown & Bigelow. In 1944 Buddy was old enough to pose for such a calendar. For the occasion his father gave him a haircut. ("That was the last time he did that. Dad had to admit that saving the 35¢ just wasn't worth the sorry results!") and the calendar was published in 1945. Although Buddy never bothered joining up himself, he was to become America's most familiar Boy Scout. 🍎

I Will Do My Best. Original oil painting for Boy Scout poster-calendar. © 1945 Brown & Bigelow, Inc., a Division of Saxon Industries, Inc. Collection Boy Scouts of America.

A *Guiding Hand.* Original oil painting for Boy Scout poster-calendar. © 1946 Brown & Bigelow, Inc., a Division of Saxon Industries, Inc. Collection Boy Scouts of America.

During his career as a Boy Scout, Buddy Edgerton was accompanied by other troopers along the way. Norman Rockwell's middle son Tommy was still Cub Scout age when he posed with Buddy for the 1946 calendar. Two years later the Edgerton boy was still appropriate for the Boy Scout, but the Cub Scout had outgrown his part and was replaced by younger brother Peter Rockwell. (In this 1948 calendar, Peter is shown gazing up at several versions of Buddy Edgerton.) Although Buddy outgrew his role as Boy Scout after this calendar and was replaced by Freeman Grout, he did return as a patrol leader in a 1966 calendar. Rockwell, having already moved to Stockbridge by then, phoned the twenty-nine-year-old Edgerton to ask if he would model for three of four profiles in the picture and to bring down his son to pose for the fourth. For the painting Rockwell added ten years to Buddy in order to create the Scout Master, removed ten years to create the Boy Scout, and inserted the Edgerton son Jimmy (whom Rockwell had never met) as the Cub Scout. "Norman insisted on giving us a check for a good deal more than $5.00 for the trouble," Buddy Edgerton recalls, "though we would have gladly done it for him without any pay."

Men of Tomorrow. Original oil painting for Boy Scout poster-calendar. © 1948 Brown & Bigelow, Inc., a Division of Saxon Industries, Inc. Collection Boy Scouts of America.

Growth of a Leader. Original oil painting for Boy Scout poster-calendar. © 1966 Brown & Bigelow, Inc., a Division of Saxon Industries, Inc. Collection Boy Scouts of America.

The youngest of the Edgerton children, Ardis, posed for the *Soldier's Homecoming* when she was eleven. She had always been a rough-and-ready, energetic child, and when Rockwell asked her to be the excited girl standing on the porch, he intended for her to pose naturally. He had expected Ardis to arrive at the studio in her everyday clothing with her red hair characteristically disheveled. Proud that the illustrator had asked her

to pose, Ardis decided to put on her Sunday best for the occasion. She combed her hair neatly, slipped into a pair of new shoes, and wore a pretty dress. Fortunately, she lived only a stone's throw from the studio, so Rockwell could send her home to change without losing much time.

The painting, which *Post* editor Ben Hibbs considered his favorite Rockwell, included some other familiar Arlington faces: on the porch Ardis Edgerton stands between Jenny McKee and Yvonne Cross, with Norman Rockwell behind them gaping at the soldier. To their right, peering from the doorway, stand the Rockwells' cook, Elizabeth LaBombard, and her husband Albert. Billie Brown, who posed for a number of Four Seasons calendars with Yvonne Cross, is shown leaping from the porch. The dog, Spot, belonged to Buddy Edgerton. Irene Hoyt, the daughter of Rose Hoyt appearing in *The*

Four Freedoms, is beaming at her returning soldier, posed by John Cross, Jr., whose father, John Sr., is smiling from the rooftop. Only after publication was it pointed out to Rockwell that Mr. Cross had no ladder to the roof.

The setting for *Soldier's Homecoming* was Troy, New York, a nearby city from which Rockwell had frequently taken the train to New York City. Peter Rockwell, accompanying his father to Troy in search for the ideal backyard for the painting, remembers that Rockwell went directly to a section of town along the railroad tracks to find what he was looking for. As a youngster, Peter always assumed his father knew where to find these things. "He always seemed to have a sense." ❧

Soldier's Homecoming. Original oil painting for a *Saturday Evening Post* cover, May 26, 1945. Collection Mrs. Ben Hibbs.

THE SCHAFERS

When Chris and Mary Schafer came to Arlington in 1947, they fantasized a life very different from the one they had left at North Shore, Chicago. Still shaken by the shock of the war years, they sought an honest environment where they could raise their children in an atmosphere promising greater connection to fundamental human values. What better way to put this fantasy into actuality than to take up dairy farming in New England? They bought the farm from George Hughes in 1948, and set right to work. Only in retrospect could they appreciate their naivete. Pastoral life did not conform to their romantic picture; this banker and his wife were unprepared for the hardships of tending fifty cows, especially with the difficulties of finding experienced farm hands to help with the daily chores.

Nevertheless, the Schafers discovered in Arlington a community of friends that more closely approximated what they had hoped to find. George and Casey Hughes introduced them to the others in the area and before long an active social life ensued. "Any event was an excuse for a party," said Mary Schafer. "Bastille day, a birthday; why, we had the most wonderful gatherings!" It probably surprised the cosmopolitan Schafers that the artists—each having been exposed to so little formal education—were well informed on a wide variety of topics. George Hughes and Jack Atherton knew so much about music; Norman Rockwell was familiar with subjects

ranging from baseball to literature. Conversation never faltered. The convivial atmosphere for these occasions was enhanced by Norman Rockwell's keen sense of humor and his talents as a raconteur. Nor did Rockwell's gift as an actor go unnoticed by this group. When Dorothy Canfield Fisher's 1920s play, "Tourists Accommodated," was revived at the Arlington Library, Norman Rockwell and Mary Schafer played the parts of husband and wife in the production. ("He was terrific," the Schafers agreed.)

Mary Schafer was particularly fond of party games—charades, word games, twenty questions—and she recalled that Rockwell's wit and intelligence sharpened these antics. She especially remembered one called "The Game." The players simply wrote on a sheet of paper what he or she most liked and most disliked. The sheets of paper were then distributed and each player was to guess who had written which. Norman Rockwell's were most telling. What he liked most: checks in the mail. What he liked least: the extra edges of white paper perforated around a sheet of new postage stamps.

In 1951 Chris Schafer received a phone call from Rockwell's assistant, Gene Pelham, urging Schafer to lend his skills as a banker by looking over the illustrator's financial records. "The books are in an awful mess," Pelham lamented, "and the Rockwells sure could use your help."

The books *were* in an awful mess, Schafer discovered. It appeared that Rockwell, who wrote checks for everything, and wrote *many* of them during the course of a week, didn't bother to balance his accounts or to record the

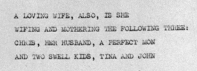

A LOVING WIFE, ALSO, IS SHE
WIFING AND MOTHERING THE FOLLOWING THREE:
CHRIS, HER HUSBAND, A PERFECT MON
AND TWO SWELL KIDS, TINA AND JOHN

WE LOVE HER FOR HER WONDROUS LOOKS
AND FOR THE THINGS SHE'S LEARNED FROM BOOKS
BUT BOOKS ALONE AREN'T NECESSARY
TO ONE SO BRIGHT AS OUR OWN MARY

HAIL MARY, MARY FULL OF GRACE
ALL ARLINGTON'S A HAPPY PLACE
HIP HIP HOORAY AND GLORY BE,
FOR MARY'S JUST TURNED TWENTY*THREE

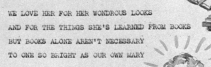

•3•

On the occasion of Mary Schafer's birthday, Norman Rockwell wrote and illustrated a poem that expressed his sentiments about his Arlington friend. Courtesy Chris and Mary Schafer.

checks in his checkbook. Schafer found that Rockwell had actually paid his federal income taxes twice that year without realizing it! It required considerable effort for Chris Schafer, even with all his financial expertise, to straighten out these records and it seemed pointless to return the books to the hopeless Rockwell systems. Schafer agreed to work for Rockwell two days a week, an arrangement that continued after the Rockwells moved to Stockbridge. "Rockwell preferred to stay in his studio and paint, untroubled by these annoying details," Schafer commented.

In the studio, Schafer would work while Rockwell painted—each man silently absorbed in his work—until the illustrator signaled the time for a break, lighting his pipe, telling a story, then returning to work after this brief interlude. Later in the day they might head for a game of tennis on the court behind the house.

Schafer assumed responsibility for most of Rockwell's business matters. When Rockwell served on the board at the Famous Artists Schools, Schafer went to Connecticut to represent Rockwell; Schafer managed his affairs while the Rockwells traveled. By the time the Rockwells moved to Stockbridge in 1953, Chris Schafer had given up farming entirely and had returned to banking, a field to which he was far better suited. He drove the two hours to Stockbridge once or twice a week, entering Rockwell's studio at 8:00 A.M., about the same time as the illustrator began his day's work at the easel, and returning to Arlington in the afternoon.

The Schafers had two children—John and Christina (whom Rockwell erroneously called "Trina" instead of "Tina" for as long as he knew her, an appellation the family accepted affectionately). John Schafer volunteered for the Peace Corps shortly after the program was initiated, and was given a teaching assignment in Ethiopia. Rockwell, who laughingly suggested the recruit might return with an Ethiopian princess, was eager to accept when the young man offered an invitation to visit Ethiopia, and took this opportunity to illustrate the Peace Corps story for *Look* magazine. Rockwell and his wife (by this time he was married to Molly) flew into Ethiopia, stayed with John Schafer, and traveled deep into the Blue Nile region where probably only few white men had ever been seen. Although Schafer's village was not used for the *Look* article, Rockwell did rely on the young man for the cover of that June 14, 1966 issue. By that time John Schafer had returned to the United States and was attending Harvard University. Rockwell asked him to come down to Stockbridge to pose for him and to bring as many other former Peace Corps recruits as he could manage to round up at Harvard. Typically Rockwell, the profiles he asked John Schafer to select for the cover were of those who had actually served. No other portraits would have been sufficiently authentic for him.

Charcoal drawing illustration by George Hughes. Collection Chris and Mary Schafer.
Photo Frank Forward.

Two original oil paintings for illustrations by George Hughes. Collection Chris and Mary Schafer.
Photos Frank Forward.

Rockwell's friends, Chris and Mary Schafer, had just the cosmopolitan air required for the stylish stories George Hughes illustrated. After buying the farm from Hughes, the Schafers had settled into their pastoral lives in Arlington, effectively weaned from Chicago's North Shore. With the proper costume and in the appropriate setting they could still be transformed into the casual sophisticates Hughes preferred for his illustrations. Chris Schafer's gray hair displayed a certain degree of distinction, favoring his portrayal as a mature lover, or a gentlemanly father. Likewise, Mary Schafer played mother and lover in Hughes's pictures. Happily, with the right clothing and appropriate hair styling, daughter Tina was equally desirable for the sophisticated set, as was her brother John. ❧

Norman Rockwell kept up his association with the Schafers for many years, a fact well chronicled by the pictures he made of the family from the time the children were quite young until their son returned from the Peace Corps in the 1960s. At Rockwell's invitation, John Schafer recruited several of his classmates at Harvard—former Peace Corps workers like himself—to pose for Rockwell in Stockbridge. In the painting, John Schafer was placed at the center of the group. ("By including John F. Kennedy," the Schafers noted, "Norman made it a totally Harvard painting.") During the course of their friendship, Rockwell asked Mary Schafer to pose for an advertisement for Dexadril, the tranquilizer, asking her to assume a rather nervous posture for the drawing. When he gave her the drawing as a gift, he wrote at the bottom, "Don't worry Mary, we all love you." ❧

The Peace Corps Led by Kennedy. Original oil painting for a *Look* cover, June 14, 1966.

THE NEIGHBORS

From his neighbors around him, Rockwell found a cast of characters that was as rich and varied as any group could be. There were two and three generations of several families that provided much material for the illustrator. There were the Crofuts, Hoyts, Brushes, Crosses, Marshes, Deckers, Squires, McKees, Martins, and Benedicts. Then there were individuals to whom he turned (many more than once) for illustrations: Carl Hess, Billie Brown, Alvie Robertson, George Zimmer, Nip Noyes, Lucille Towne, Dr. George Russell, Roy Cole, Frank Hall, Floyd Bentley. Rockwell was never at a loss for the right "type." A call from Rockwell meant a match was being made between idea and actuality—and the neighbors stood ready to serve. "It made you feel important," said Doris Crofut Wright.

Although the entire community anticipated publication of a *Post* cover— knowing one of them was likely to appear—little fuss was made about the man who created these popular images. He was—as were the writer Dorothy Canfield Fisher, the composer Charles Ruggles, and the artist Grandma Moses who all lived nearby—simply a neighbor. "He was one of us," said Mrs. Brush. "He never put on airs."

Willie Gillis with Food Package. Saturday Evening Post cover, October 4, 1941.

Willie Gillis Asleep. Saturday Evening Post cover, November 29, 1941.

Willie Gillis at the U.S.O. Saturday Evening Post cover, February 7, 1942.

Willie Gillis in Church. Saturday Evening Post cover, July 25, 1942.

Arguing Over Willie Gillis. Saturday Evening Post cover, September 5, 1942.

Even before Pearl Harbor, Norman Rockwell thought it would be interesting to do a series of paintings about one soldier. The young man's experiences in combat would tell a story that all readers would appreciate, and through him Rockwell would create a lovable warrior in a variety of settings. For the paintings Rockwell would need someone likely to remain in the area for the duration of the series. He found Robert Otis Buck where he had found so many other Arlington models, at a square dance held at West Arlington's Grange Hall. Buck had just the sort of innocent look Rockwell wanted for the part, and Buck was exempt from the draft.

For the first painting in the series Rockwell posed Jim Edgerton and Gene Pelham behind Bob Buck, the men following an appetizing package from home. Needing a name for the address label on the package, Rockwell consulted his wife Mary. She thought up the name Willie Gillis after a book she had read to the children called *Wee Willie Winkie*.

The series got off to a bumpy start: attentive *Post* readers pointed out that the Gillis package from home contained insufficient postage (after that Rockwell weighed in his packages at the post office before he painted any stamps), and some real Willie Gillises began to surface. Rockwell remembered one—a colonel who was later promoted to brigadier general.

Ben Hibbs became Editor of the *Post* after four Gillis covers had been completed, and he urged Rockwell to continue.

Although he had been exempted from the draft, Bob Buck felt he could not simply stay at home while a war was going on. To his dismay, Rockwell lost his Willie Gillis in 1943, when Buck enlisted as a naval aviator and flew off to the Pacific. Lacking a real model, the illustrator was forced to improvise if he wanted to keep the series going. In the next cover, he used photographs of Bob Buck when he painted Lee Schaeffer sleeping through New Year's Eve. 🍎

Willie Gillis on K.P. Saturday Evening Post cover, April 11, 1942.

Willie Gillis in a Blackout. Saturday Evening Post cover, June 27, 1942.

Willie Gillis with an Indian Fakir. Saturday Evening Post cover, June 26, 1943.

New Year's Eve Without Willie Gillis. Saturday Evening Post cover, January 1, 1944.

With Bob Buck off at war, Rockwell devised clever methods of continuing the Willie Gillis series without the model present. The illustrator was particularly proud of his ingenuity with this painting. Working from head-shots he had taken before Buck's departure, Rockwell created six generations of fighting Gillises. He had a fine time with this *trompe l'oeil* still life. He switched around the head gear, careful to retain the accuracy of the historic costumes, and he fabricated a complete library of tomes documenting the military valor of the Gillis family. Pleased with his imaginative solution to the Gillis problem, he lamented at the public response: "The cover was very popular, mostly, I'm sorry to say, because of those books. All the Gillises in America wrote to me asking where they could buy them."

The Fighting Gillises. Original oil painting for a *Saturday Evening Post* cover, September 16, 1944. Collection Mr. and Mrs. Ken Stuart.

Willie Gillis in College. Original oil painting for a *Saturday Evening Post* cover, October 5, 1946. Courtesy Phillips Fine Art Auctioneers, New York.

R ockwell wasn't obliged to improvise any more
Willie Gillis covers without Bob Buck present to
pose. Not long after his last ingenious effort with the
Gillis series, the war ended and Bob Buck returned to
Arlington. For the final cover in the Gillis sequence,
Rockwell sent his subject to college. Starting with a
whole host of props to tell the story, Rockwell eventually
edited them down to only a few: the helmet, insignia,
document, books, and golf clubs were sufficient to
describe where Willie had been and where he was going.
Naturally, Rockwell had to get the view from the college
dormitory just right, so he went off to nearby Williams
College to photograph the collegiate bell tower for the
painting.

Four Freedoms: Freedom of Worship.

Four Freedoms: Freedom of Speech.

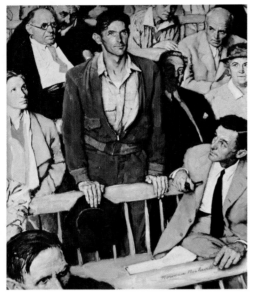

Freedom of Speech. Original oil painting for poster, 1943. The Metropolitan Museum of Art, New York. George A. Hearn Fund, 1952.

Discouraged in their efforts to contribute their services to the government during World War II, Mead Schaeffer and Norman Rockwell went to Philadelphia to discuss their ideas with Ben Hibbs at the *Post*. As a result of this meeting, Hibbs commissioned Rockwell to do *The Four Freedoms*, a project to which the illustrator devoted a full six months.

Freedom of Speech

Rockwell began the series with *Freedom of Speech*, starting it over four times before he arrived at the final concept. The idea originated from a town meeting where Jim Edgerton rose to state his opinion of the proposed construction for the new Arlington High School replacing the old one that had recently burned down. Rockwell was impressed by the respect for controversy evident at the meeting and he rushed home to sketch out his new idea.

Carl Hess had never posed for Rockwell before. Except for the times the illustrator filled his tank at Hess's gas station, Hess hardly knew him. ("My kids went to school with his kids, and his wife came to the station often, but I didn't have much contact with Norman Rockwell himself.") It was Rockwell's assistant, Gene Pelham, who thought of Hess for the central figure in the painting, and Rockwell wholeheartedly agreed with the choice.

In an earlier version, Rockwell placed all the figures sitting squarely around Hess. (In this version Dr. Russell is seated to the left behind Hess.) Although Carl Hess preferred this version ("looked more natural," he said), Rockwell felt there were too many people in the picture. "It was too diverse, it went every which way and didn't settle anywhere or say anything," Rockwell reported. Instead, he took a view below eye level as if he too were sitting on a bench looking up—a far more dramatic expression.

In fact, any of these individuals could have participated in that town meeting in Arlington. In the lower left corner is the ear of Carl Hess's father, Henry. Jim Martin is in the lower right corner with Harry Brown (Billie Brown's father) immediately above him. To the left of Carl Hess is Robert Benedict, Sr. (father of Robert, Jr. who owned the Benedict's Garage seen in the *Post* cover of October 13, 1945). Seated alongside Mr. Benedict is Rose Hoyt, a face more prominent in *Freedom of Worship*. To add interest to the left edge of the composition, Rockwell placed his own eye, a characteristic touch of the artist.

Freedom of Worship

The next in the series took two months to complete. Rockwell was inspired by a saying, "Each according to the dictates of his own conscience," but had no idea where he had seen it. Mary Rockwell hunted for it, and he asked every model who came to pose, but the source was never located. It's possible he made it up.

Rose Hoyt's braided hair crowned her head, and she was three months pregnant when she came to pose for *Freedom of Worship*. On a wall of his studio Rockwell had tacked a line drawing with cut-out photographs of profiles dropped into place on the drawing. When Mrs. Hoyt arrived, he explained the idea for *Freedom of Worship*, pointing out which profile in the drawing had been designated for her. "Knowing I was a Protestant, he asked if I minded posing as a Catholic, and I assured him I had no objection. That pleased him because he felt the rosary was important to his picture. But it was thoughtful of him to ask." She posed for three sessions before he finally got exactly what he wanted in the photograph.

The others in the painting include Mrs. Harrington; Walter Squires (Rockwell's carpenter, who also appeared in *The Forging Contest* and *Spirit of Kansas City*); Squires' wife Clara at the right-hand edge; Winfield Secoy and Jim Martin in the center.

"We had no idea the painting would become so important. Somehow we all took it for granted. It was just something you did."

Appearing in both *Freedom of Speech* and *Freedom of Worship* made Rose Hoyt very proud, and she was touched by Rockwell's portrayal of her, as if he'd seen something special. "I never thought of myself as being beautiful," Mrs. Hoyt said. But Rockwell certainly did.

Freedom from Want

The next two went far more easily. On Thanksgiving Day Rockwell photographed his cook, Mrs. Wheaton, laying out the turkey for the family. ("Our cook cooked it, I painted it, and we ate it," said Rockwell. "That was one of the few times I've ever eaten the model.") Others in the painting include, from Mrs. Wheaton to the right: Lester Brush, Florence Lindsey, Norman Rockwell's mother, Jim Martin, Mr. Wheaton, Mary Rockwell, Charles Lindsey, the Hoisington children. (Shirley Hoisington beat up Peter Rockwell in the sixth grade—sat on him, in fact—as the victim himself reported.)

Freedom from Fear

Perhaps because he had so little difficulty with this painting, Rockwell was never pleased with it, nor, for that matter, was he partial to *Freedom from Want* either. *Freedom from Fear* "was based on a rather smug idea. Painted during the bombing of London, it was supposed to say, 'Thank God we can put our children to bed with a feeling of security, knowing they will not be killed in the night.'"

Jim Martin was the model for the father, Mrs. Edgar Lawrence the mother, and the two children of carpenter Walt Squires performed the role of the sleeping pair.

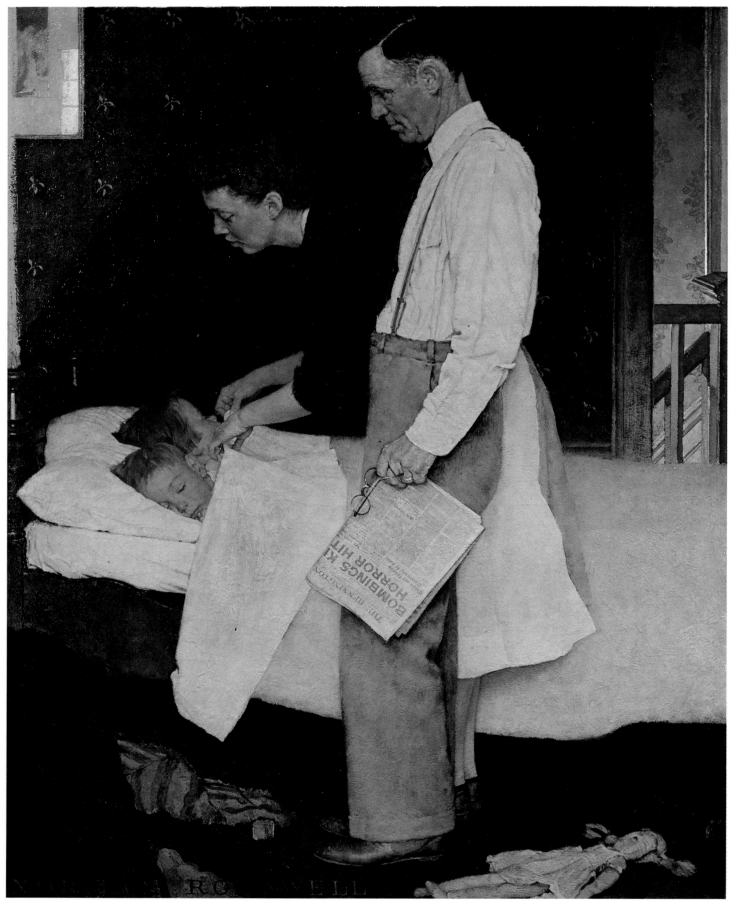

Four Freedoms: Freedom from Fear.

All original oil paintings for a government war bond program, 1943. Old Corner House Collection, Stockbridge, Massachusetts.

Four Freedoms: Freedom from Want.

It wasn't always easy for a model to know whether a session of posing would result in a published illustration. Rockwell frequently discarded an idea along the way or replaced one model with another. Even if he managed to complete a painting entirely (as he did this one), he might still abandon it in favor of another idea. No wonder a model could lose track of an illustration.

Although this painting was not used for the *Post* cover for which it was intended, it has nevertheless become almost as familiar as the one published on the April 29, 1944 issue. (George Zimmer posed for the published version.) Perhaps the unpublished work is the superior painting. It was certainly an example of Rockwell's early experiments with a more subtle painting technique. "He experimented a lot," said Peter Rockwell. "Here he started to get some of the colors and qualities of Dutch painting. He used the same techniques: underpainting in sepia, adding color, glazing and scumbling the surface as the Dutch masters did."

To authenticate this interior of Comar's Diner, Rockwell used Mr. Comar himself behind the counter. Walt Smith, a shop owner in West Arlington, posed for the gentleman wearing eyeshades. Duane Peters, the young marine telling the war stories in Benedict's Garage (*Post*, October 13, 1945) is posed here in uniform, and the small hunched figure holding the knife, Albert LaBombard, was the husband of Rockwell's cook. 🦃

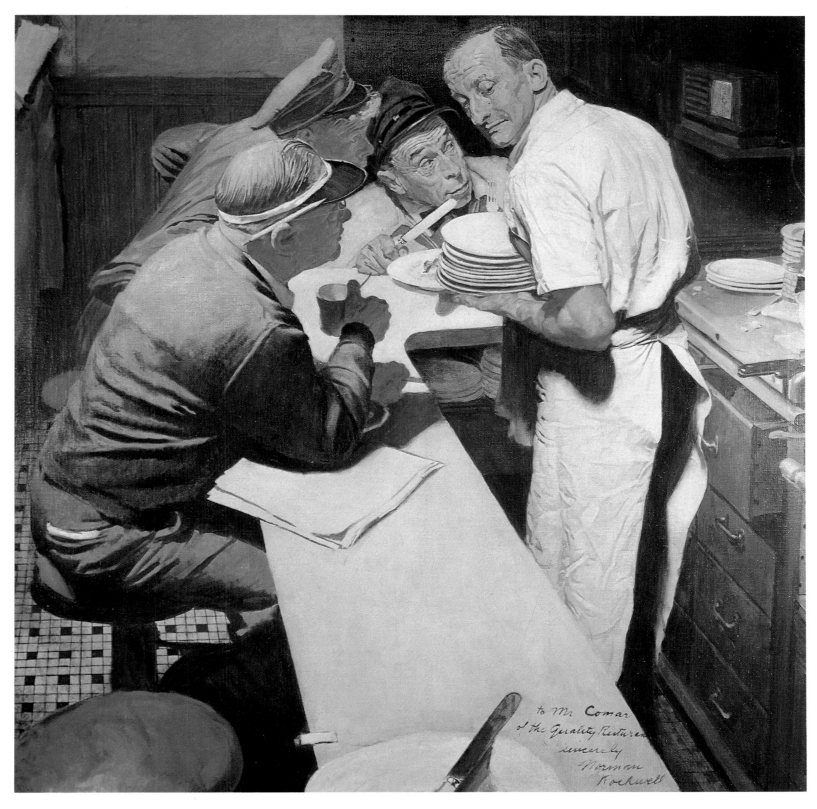

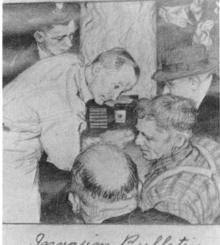

Listening for the Invasion of D-Day. Original oil painting for Mr. Comar of the Quality Restaurant, Manchester, Vermont. Old Corner House Collection, Stockbridge, Massachusetts.

Listening for the Invasion of D-Day (final version). *Saturday Evening Post* cover, April 29, 1944.

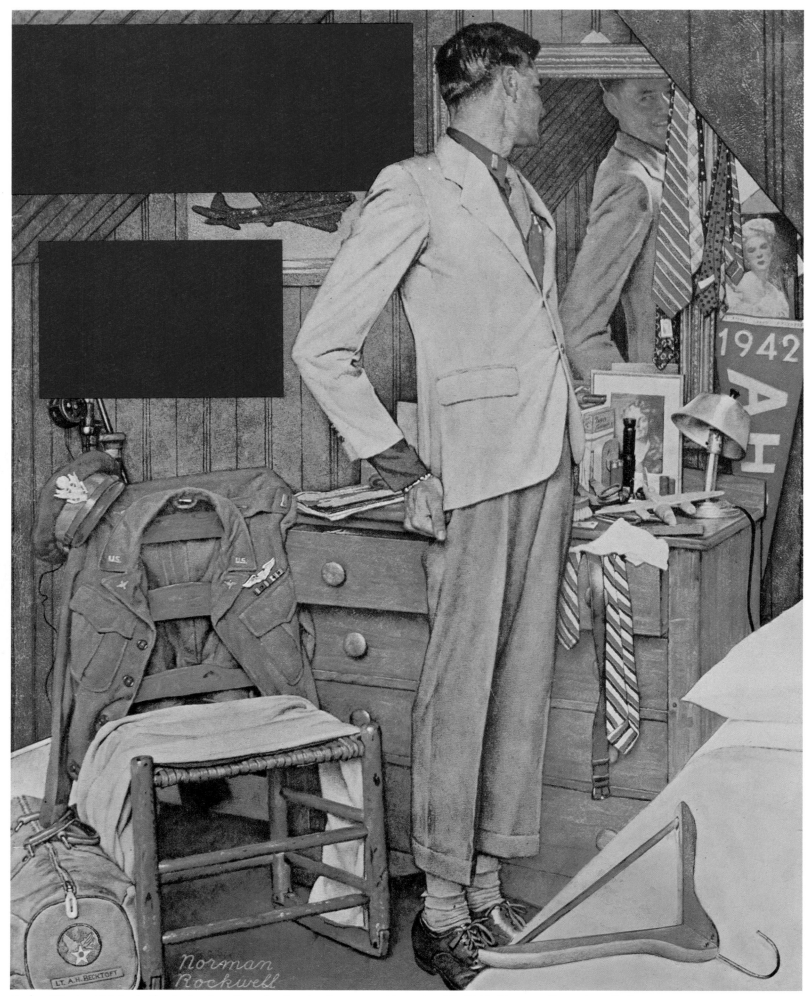

Back to Civvies. Original oil painting for a *Saturday Evening Post* cover, December 15, 1945. Courtesy Danenberg Gallery.

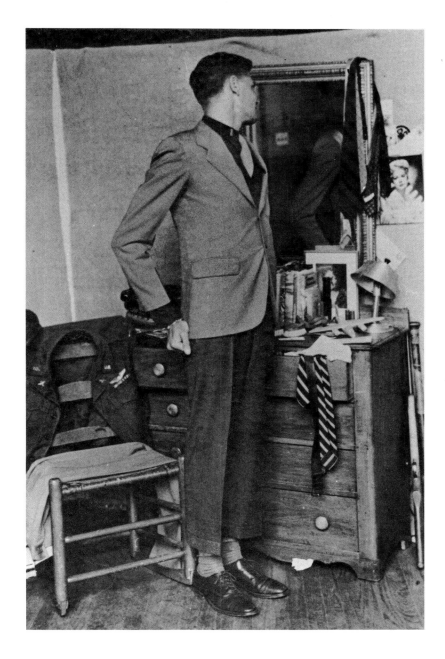

The theme of the returning soldier was one Rockwell used in a variety of forms. Bob Buck had not yet returned to Arlington, but Art Becktoft, an air pilot who had spent many months in a prison camp, was home now and gave Rockwell the ideal model for the over-sized civilian. Rockwell had no difficulty gathering a wardrobe of under-sized clothes, but he made his final selection only after trying on some outfits himself and having others do the same. Becktoft's uniform and satchel provided the authentic props. 🍎

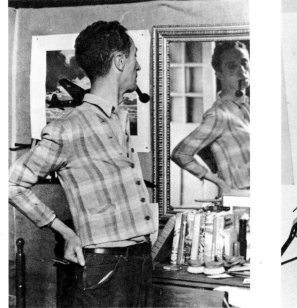

The Horseshoe Forging Contest. Original oil painting as illustration for the story "Blacksmith's Boy—Heel and Toe" by Edward W. O'Brien, *Saturday Evening Post,* November 2, 1940. Old Corner House Collection, Stockbridge, Massachusetts.

Only a few miles from Arlington in South Shaftsbury, Vermont, stood Moon's Blacksmith Shop which boasted on its sign: "Practical and artistic horse-shoeing." (Today the location is a vacant lot.) Rockwell's drawing of the shop was made from his visit there. The models were photographed individually in the studio that later burned down. Walt Squires, the carpenter who would build Rockwell's new studio three years later, posed for one of the blacksmiths. (His large physique was just as suitable for the *Spirit of Kansas City.*) Divided equally down the center to allow for the gutter separating the double-page illustration, the composition is framed by an array of Arlington "types" looking in and out of the picture in a cleverly designed grouping. Locking eyes with the viewer on the lower left is Arlington's under-

sheriff, Harvey McKee, with his distinctive mustache. ("He hadn't shaved his mustache since he was twenty-one," his son reported recently.) On the right, McKee's mustache has been removed by Rockwell's brush and the under-sheriff—with the cigarette between his lips—is virtually unrecognizable. Instead, the mustache was given to the barelipped Nip Noyes, in the bowler above McKee, then removed again for the Nip Noyes immediately below the same figure. Henry Hess (of *Freedom of Speech*) is in the lower right corner, and Clarence Decker (*Strictly a Sharpshooter* and *The Tattooist*) posed for one of the figures in the group at the upper left. Norman Rockwell peers at the viewer through the group at the left. ❦

Rockwell took no short cuts when it came to establishing the authentic setting for a picture. The textures, architectural details, lighting—the very *atmosphere* of an environment had to be right. For *Charwomen*, he arranged a photography session in Broadway's Majestic Theatre. Between performances of the musical *Carousel* the theater was empty and the illustrator was free to explore all the theatrical details that would make the painting convincing. The original concept of a cleaning woman playing the grand piano in rapture seemed exaggerated. Two women absorbed in reading the program after hours seemed more convincing and, at the same time, provided the artist an opportunity to work with a strong, simple composition. Rockwell was a master at using compositional devices that direct the viewer to the central story. Here the two women are framed by a sea of reds, encircled by delicately placed seat markers, and centered between the deliberate lines of two broomstick handles. Without seeming contrived, the selection and placement of these elements reinforce the story.

Back at the studio, Rockwell selected two Arlington neighbors for the final picture: Jenny McKee, the wife of under-sheriff Harvey McKee, is seated at the left, and alongside her is Mrs. Charles Crofut, whose family is presented on the following picture spread.

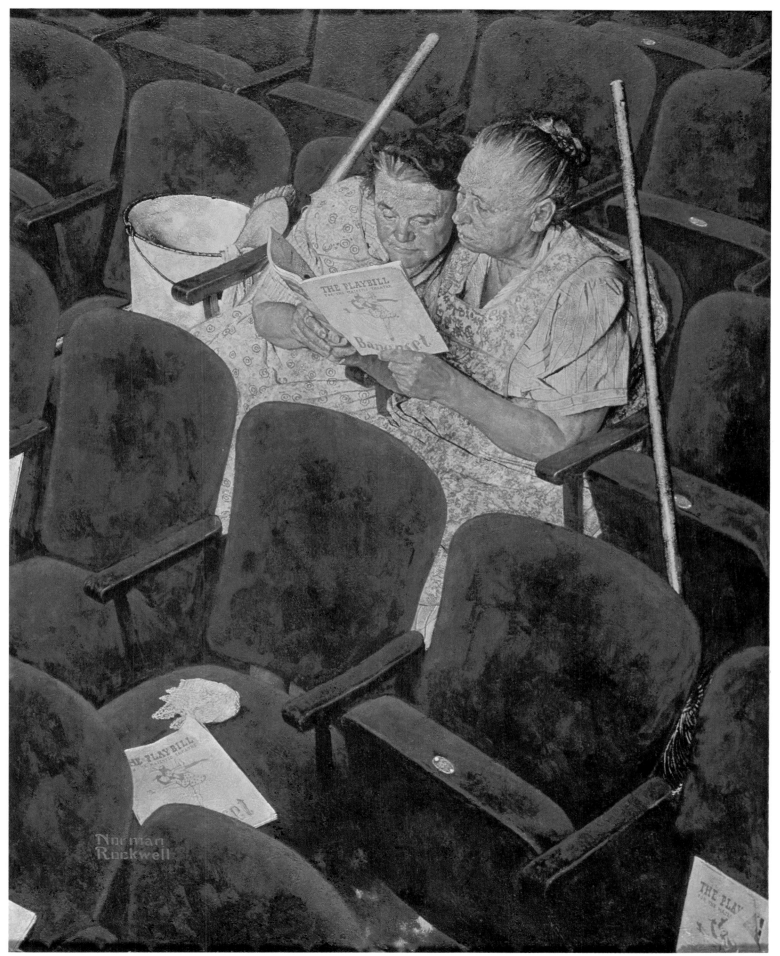

Charwomen. Original oil painting for a *Saturday Evening Post* cover, April 6, 1946. Collection Newell J. Ward, Jr.

Illustrations from Four Seasons Calendars. © 1948 and 1955 Brown & Bigelow, Inc., a Division of Saxon Industries, Inc.

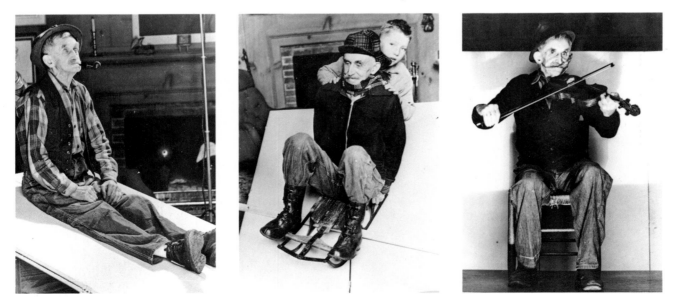

Charles Crofut was not very different in real life from the way he was portrayed by Norman Rockwell in the Four Seasons calendars. Almost as spry at seventy-five as he had been as a young man, Mr. Crofut enjoyed roaming the Vermont countryside, fishing and hunting. Posing with young Billie Brown and with a neighbor's dog named Gent, Charles Crofut was eager to please the illustrator, but Rockwell was cautious not to let the elderly gentleman overexert himself for these vigorous poses. Charles Crofut's wife had posed for *Charwomen* and his daughter-in-law and granddaughter Doris posed for *The Gossips*. His grandson, Roy Crofut, was a handsome young lad who posed with Janet Cross for one of the Four Ages of Love in the 1955 Brown & Bigelow Four Seasons calendar. Rockwell took a liking to Roy Crofut and managed to find odd jobs for the boy to do during the winter when he knew money was short. Crofut cleaned out the Rockwells' cellar, garage, and corn house, and on two occasions delivered pictures to Curtis in Philadelphia. "Be sure to tip everyone," Rockwell told Crofut before departure, handing him sufficient money for an overnight stay in New York. "When I arrived in the city everyone seemed to know Norman Rockwell—the redcaps in Penn Station and the bellboys at the hotel all jumped to help me with the big package because they knew how generous he was."

Charles Crofut.

Mrs. Charles Crofut.

Rena Crofut.

Doris Crofut.

Roy Crofut.

The office of Dr. George Russell in Arlington, Vermont, was a familiar room. Prior to photographing, Rockwell straightened up the place considerably, without destroying the warmth and reassurance associated with the office. Dr. Russell was beloved in Arlington for his paternal bedside manner and his devotion to his patients. He was also an avid collector of "Vermontiana," memorabilia from Old Vermont, which he proudly displayed. The medical equipment in the office, comical by contemporary standards, is well remembered by the Rockwell offspring: an electrical contraption shown at the right, which was used to remove a few warts from Tommy's hand ("I got an awful electric shock from the thing"), and an X-ray machine "which would probably violate every radiation code today," laughed Peter Rockwell. Dr. Russell never actually gave up his practice, although he made several attempts to do so. "Patients just wouldn't let him retire," Marie Briggs remarked.

Rockwell knew he wanted to paint a family with Dr. Russell and with the Russell dog Bozo, and he had two photographic sessions for the painting with his good friend Ann Marsh and two of her sons. But Rockwell wasn't satisfied with his composition. With much effort, he arrived at a better idea and called Ann Marsh to see if she could pose that day. "My son Chuck was in New Hampshire which meant I couldn't get him back to Arlington until the next day. But Norman could be impulsive—once he made up his mind that was it, and he just couldn't wait that long!"

Mr. and Mrs. Larry Brush were delighted to oblige when Rockwell called them. "He asked us to dress our baby in a romper suit for the picture," Mrs. Brush remembered. "I guess it comes as a surprise for people to hear that the child in the blue romper is actually a girl!" The family portrait became even more treasured to the Brushes only a few years later when their son John, pictured at the right, was tragically drowned in a lake attempting to save another boy's life. ❧

Visit to a Country Doctor. Original oil painting for a *Saturday Evening Post* series, April 12, 1947. Old Corner House Collection, Stockbridge, Massachusetts.

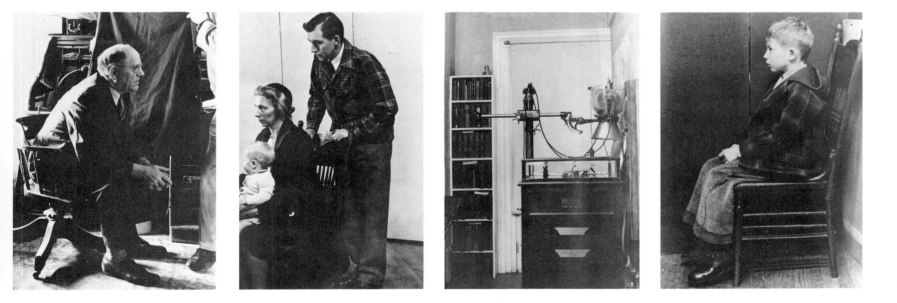

East Arlington, where Shuffleton's Barbershop was located before a grocery chain took over the building, lies just on the other side of Arlington, one small street containing only a couple of shops and a post office. This is an unlikely location for what has come to be considered one of Rockwell's most outstanding achievements, possibly the finest example of pure painting ever to appear on the cover of any magazine. Rockwell was fascinated with the complex challenge of painting a lighted room through a dark room, and through a window. Only the *Saturday Evening Post* could provide Rockwell with a vehicle for stretching his artistic capabilities. And it is to his credit that Norman Rockwell took advantage of this opportunity, although he was so badly pressed by the pressures of deadlines from other clients. The painting demonstrates Rockwell's admiration for the Dutch painters—Vermeer in particular—

who delighted in painting the play of light within a darkened room. (Peter Rockwell remembered how proud his father was years later when he figured out exactly the window in Delft that Vermeer must have painted from.) Don Spaulding, who regards *Shuffleton's Barbershop* as Rockwell's finest painting, recalled the illustrator talking about the difficulties he encountered when he worked on the painting during a particularly cloudy two- or three-month period in the fall of 1949. With the qualities of sharp light as the central interest in the painting, the diffused cloudy days were a source of constant frustration to Rockwell. "When he'd get into trouble with a painting," Spaulding recalled, "He'd go into a funk, saying 'boy, what a Palooka I turned out to be,' but by 8:30 the next morning he'd be back at it. His discipline was a real lesson to those of us who thought painting should come easily."❧

Shuffleton's Barbershop. Original oil painting for a *Saturday Evening Post* cover, April 29, 1950. Estate of Norman Rockwell.

Facts of Life. Saturday Evening Post cover, July 14, 1951.

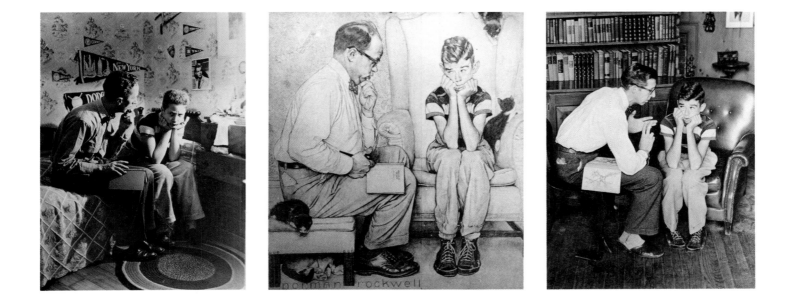

Rockwell did many versions for *Facts of Life* before he was satisfied. He asked so many friends for advice that most assumed he would eventually abandon the subject entirely. "He may just have found the subject too close to home," suggested Jarvis Rockwell.

Determining the perfect wallpaper pattern occupied much of Rockwell's energy: several styles were photographed, and a pattern—designed by Jack Atherton—was actually traced and rendered on canvas by Rockwell's apprentice Don Winslow. Rockwell ultimately changed the setting altogether, shifting the location of the intimate talk from the bedroom to the living room, and simplifying the background treatment entirely.

Rockwell also tried out other models before he selected Lester Brush for the father and Dwight Cowan for the awkward boy. "Dwight was my best friend in Arlington," recalled Peter Rockwell, "but for years my father carried on a private war with him at the dinner table. He tried to give Dwight more than he could eat, just to see if he would ever stop asking for seconds. No matter how much food Pop piled on the plate, Dwight would ask for more. And no matter how much Dwight ate, he stayed pencil thin, just as he is in this picture."

Tall and lean, Lester Brush was a natural physical match to Dwight Cowan. "Norman Rockwell said I reminded him of one of his models from New Rochelle [Fred Hildebrandt]," said Brush. (Rockwell found Lester Brush equally appealing for Scrooge in a Hallmark Christmas card and for Abe Lincoln in an educational text. Brush is also one of the gossips.) For this part, Rockwell wanted to suggest a rather well-to-do man considerably older than Brush. To convey this in clothing, Rockwell asked his model to wear a pair of comfortable, casually worn-out slippers, and he gave Brush money to buy a new white shirt. 🐛

Photo courtesy Don Spaulding.

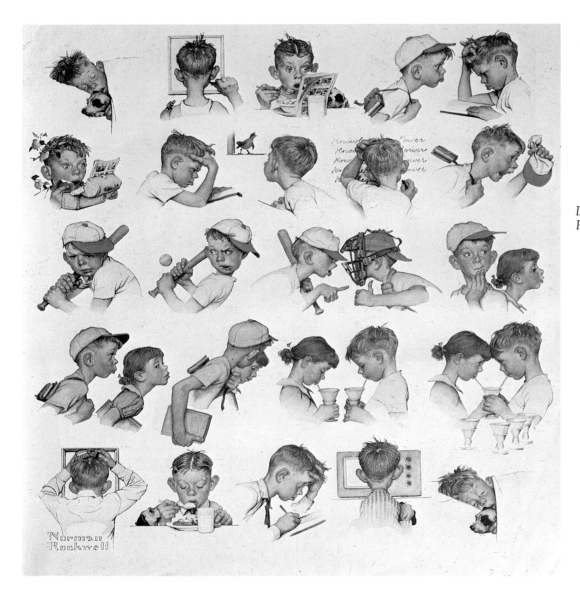

Day in a Boy's Life. Saturday Evening Post cover, May 24, 1952.

Rockwell's "keyhole approach" was used to good effect for *Day in a Boy's Life* as it had been in *The Gossips.* In need of a cute and devilish type, Rockwell selected Chuck Marsh, the oldest son of local elementary schoolteacher, Ann Marsh. (Chuck Marsh had posed for the Four Seasons calendars and for the *Family Homecoming.*) Rockwell's skills as a director were especially required for this sequence. Although the costumes provided some narrative value, the success of the cover depended almost exclusively on Chuck Marsh's expressive face.

The Rockwells felt a particular affection for the Marshes. When Chuckie was born in November, Mary Rockwell offered to baby-sit so that Lee and Ann Marsh could do their Christmas shopping, and Norman Rockwell took a creative writing course in Bennington with Mrs. Marsh. The Marshes had been at a party in the Rockwells' studio the evening it burned down in 1943. Having already returned home, they soundly slept through the howling sirens as the fire engines sped by their home in the middle of the night.

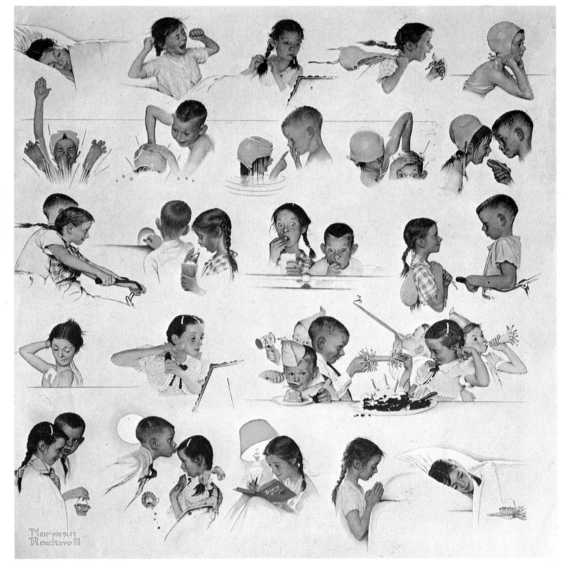

Day in a Girl's Life. Original oil painting for a *Saturday Evening Post* cover, August 30, 1952. Old Corner House Collection, Stockbridge, Massachusetts.

When Rockwell painted *Day in a Boy's Life*, he had not yet met Mary Whalen or he would have used her in that cover. He met the little girl for the first time when he attended a high school basketball game in which his son Tommy was playing. Complaining to her father that she was thirsty, Mary Whalen cheerfully accepted Norman Rockwell's offer of a sip from his Coke. The illustrator had many favorite boy models during his illustrious career, but no girl ever came as close to perfection as this expressive child who could play any part he requested. "She was the best model I ever had," he said, "could look sad one minute, jolly the next, and raise her eyebrows until they almost jumped over her head." He used her first for a Plymouth advertisement, and then many times after that. She also posed for George Hughes and for Don Winslow, but Rockwell was her favorite.

In *Day in a Girl's Life*, Mary Whalen posed with Chuck Marsh, and for the party scene she was joined by her twin brother Peter and by Chuck's brother Donny. Rockwell observed later that this cover was not as successful as *Day in a Boy's Life* had been; probably, he conjectured, "because a girl's activities are not as varied."❧

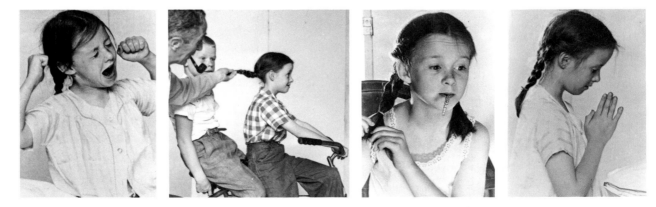

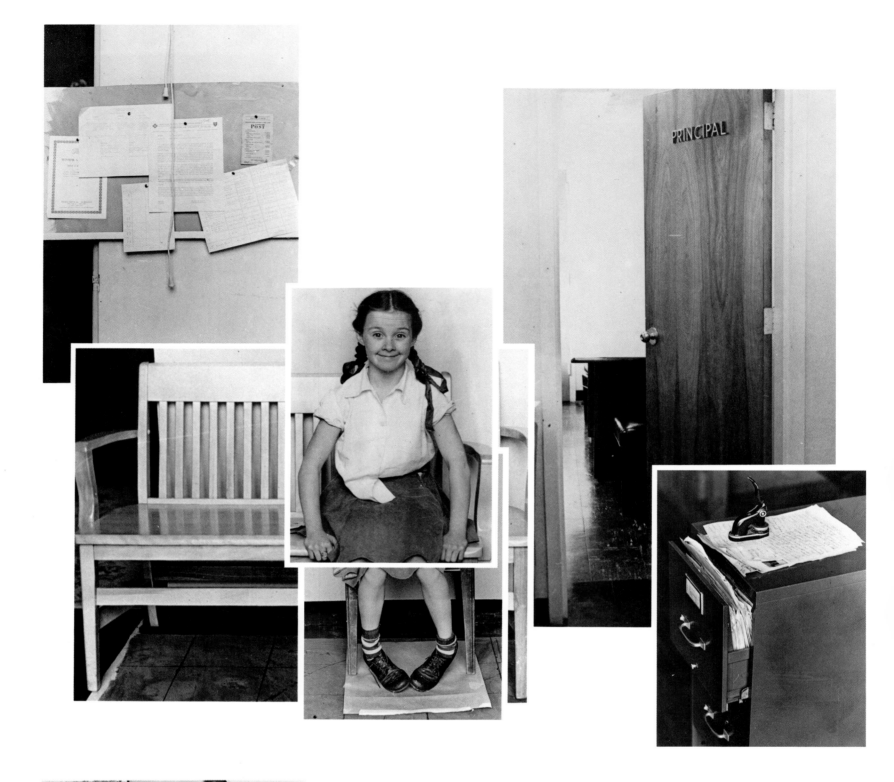

Was it necessary to put in the adults here or not? Rockwell wavered back and forth; he put them in and took them out, and put them back in. George Hughes is convinced they were retained because he advised Rockwell to remove them. Fortunately, the central figure was less problematic.

A note from the school principal awaited Mary Whalen when she returned from a fourth-grade class outing one afternoon. Frightened, she begged her twin brother Peter to accompany her to the office to see what the charges against her would be. To her relief she discovered that it was simply a message from Mr. Rockwell saying he'd arranged with her parents to pick her up that afternoon for a photo session. At the studio she found Mr. Rockwell

Outside the Principal's Office. Original oil painting for a *Saturday Evening Post* cover. May 23, 1953.

in excellent humor, laughing heartily over his funny cover idea as he showed her the sketch. ("He could be so impish," Mary Whalen recalled. "Like a child himself.") He literally rolled on the floor with laughter as he urged her to produce a big smile for the camera, and her broad, devilish grin came easily. Rockwell had greater difficulty with the feet, and spent another session photographing only her shoes and socks. But the biggest chore was the black eye. He applied charcoal over Mary Whalen's eye, without satisfaction. Then he applied makeup, but was

unable to obtain the accurate colors and uneven swelling of a real black eye. Finally, he wrote about his dilemma in the newspaper, announcing that he would pay $5.00 for a genuine black eye. The item was picked up by the wire services and overnight he was offered several hundred black eyes from prisons and football teams. He eventually selected one belonging to a boy nearby. Success was achieved when he painted the real black eye over Mary Whalen's unblemished one, giving him precisely the convincing effect he was after.

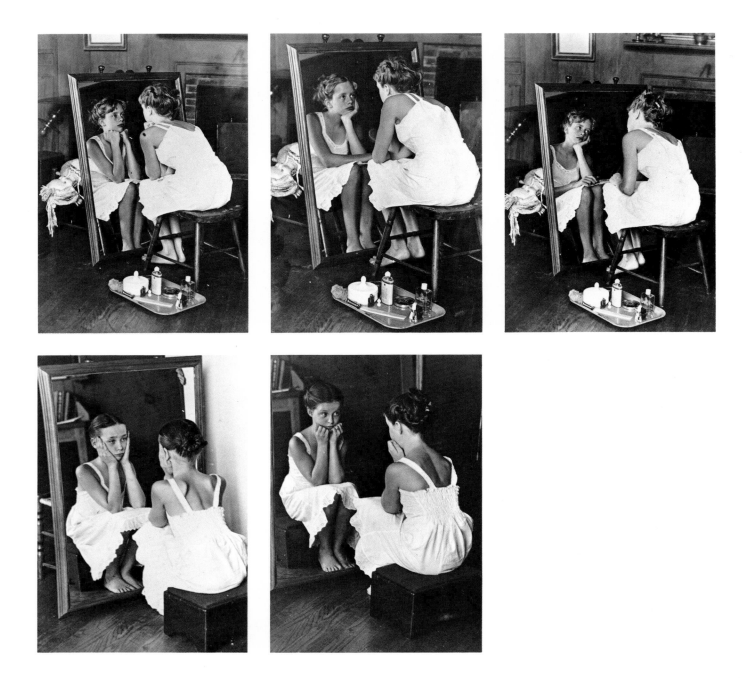

Shortly before moving to Stockbridge in 1953, Norman Rockwell photographed Mary Whalen for the *Girl at the Mirror*. He completed the painting in his new home. It was not until the magazine was published that the model ever saw the results from that single photography session. Rockwell mailed her the reproduction with a note, "I hope you like it." "Sending me the picture and letter was so typical of him," Mary Whalen observed. "It was not until years later that I realized what a special gift he had given me with this friendship. He cared about my twelve-year-old imagination. He felt that if I understood what he was trying to accomplish in a painting, the picture would be good, but if I didn't, there was something wrong with his idea. We were all in it together, somehow. At least he made me feel that way."

Although the painting became one of Rockwell's most popular covers, the artist himself was critical. In retrospect, he was sorry that he had included the magazine with Jane Russell's photograph, a distracting detail he would have edited out if he were to do the painting over. 🐦

Girl at the Mirror. Original oil painting for a *Saturday Evening Post* cover, March 6, 1954. Old Corner House Collection, Stockbridge, Massachusetts.

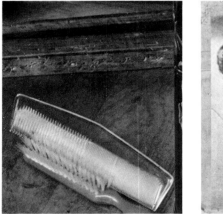

 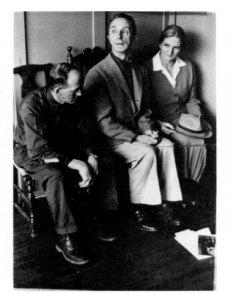 

The idea for this painting came from Rockwell's sense of loss when his eldest son Jarvis had enlisted in the Air Force and his two other boys had gone off to school. Completed in Stockbridge, the painting was begun in Arlington. Sometimes it is as interesting to consider the photographs Rockwell eliminated as it is to see the ones he finally selected. Like a series of sketches, these photographs describe the progression of his ideas, the creative process as Rockwell experienced it. The photographs reveal that he made several adjustments in the figures, eliminating the mother as an unnecessary detail along the way. (Tom Rockwell filled in for the boy in the photograph until his father made his final selection.) Floyd Bentley, an Arlington farmer and cousin to the Rockwells' cook Marie Briggs, sat for the father. The photographs demonstrate that Rockwell shifted from the running board of an old car, to the waiting area of a railroad station, and finally returned to his original concept. He indicated the railroad setting simply, by including the lantern and a slice of track in the foreground. The ideas were therefore *absorbed* into the final painting, not *eliminated* altogether.

Peter Rockwell, who had graduated from high school when Rockwell was completing this painting, remembers the problem his father had with the signature. The illustrator tried placing it under the dog, but that didn't work. He settled on the footlocker as a better location for his signature, careful to avoid any suggestion that it would appear to be lettering on the trunk. Attention to details such as this always impressed Peter Rockwell and he kept it in mind years later when he became an artist himself. ❦

Breaking Home Ties. Original oil painting for a *Saturday Evening Post* cover, September 25, 1954. Collection Don Trachte.

The Family
MODELS AT HOME

Rockwell relied frequently upon his models at home. Posing in costume with Mary Rockwell, the illustrator watched Henry Ford drive away in the first Ford automobile.

From New Rochelle to Arlington to Stockbridge, changes in geography did not seem dramatically to affect Norman Rockwell's routine. All his studios even looked alike, constructed with a large window casting its north light onto an open area, with steps leading to an open balcony overlooking the studio. Throughout the years Rockwell maintained a disciplined routine, issuing relatively constant and even output wherever he worked. Naturally, the activity of the household centered around Rockwell's professional life, his deadlines, his disappointments and triumphs, and his requirements for adequate time and space for illustration. He organized his life to permit him this freedom: his wife helped him, there was a "Man Friday" on hand, a cook, neighbors frequently hired for odd jobs and for deliveries, and in later years he hired a secretary, a business manager, and someone to drive for him on occasional trips with the car.

Rockwell never left his work far behind, even at night when he might awaken from his sleep with an idea, rushing to the studio before dawn to work it out. "He didn't have time for anything else but painting," recalled Peter Rockwell. "He painted a half day on Thanksgiving and even tried painting a half day on Christmas, until my mother put her foot down." Don Spaulding observed: "He was totally single-minded about his work. Jack Atherton once remarked that he didn't know how Norman managed to do it, never taking out the garbage or fixing a screen door. It was as if his entire life was directed to making pictures." If domestic pressures became too great, in fact, Rockwell might be likely to retreat into his studio even more frequently. "He worked out many of his conflicts through his paintings," Jarvis Rockwell commented. Where his life in the studio ended and his life outside began did become blurred, as even Rockwell himself noted: "The story of my life is, really, the story of my pictures and how I made them. Because, in one way or another, everything I have ever seen or done has gone into my pictures."

Rockwell worked every day, seven days a week, from about 8:00 in the morning until 5:00, with a break for lunch. He often returned to his studio after dinner, if only to clean his brushes or fret over a painting in progress. Even at meals, Rockwell was often absorbed in his work, preoccupied with a painting that wasn't going right, or thinking already in advance of the next commission.

Although he enjoyed parties, was a convivial storyteller, and extremely interested in those around him, he avoided the distractions of a hectic social life. He would prefer to put up his guests at the Arlington Inn rather than have them stay at the house. George Hughes remembered that even when Rockwell expected guests for dinner he worked right up to the last moment, often rushing in from the studio as the guests pulled into the driveway.

The Rockwells' tastes were simple; no need to flaunt the substantial income he earned from his illustrations. For years in Vermont the family continued to drive the old Chevy station wagon their neighbor Colonel Ayres had given Rockwell during the war when cars were scarce in exchange for painting his portrait. (The Edgertons adopted the car as a school bus when the Rockwells finally got a new automobile.) Little fuss was made over amenities of any sort. ("Norman always ate roast beef, steak, or lamb chops for dinner," Chris Schafer recalled. "Like everything else about him—basic and honest, with no pretense whatsoever.")

Rockwell was a man of habit. He would sip one Coke in the late morning and another in the afternoon (throwing half away each time), listen to the Saturday afternoon Metropolitan Opera performance or the New York Yankees baseball game on the radio. He kept the studio neat at all times, sweeping up several times during the course of a day. His wife very often read aloud to him—she was a skilled reader, having been a schoolteacher before she met Norman—including all his favorite novels by Dickens, Dostoevsky, Tolstoy. (She read *War and Peace* to him twice!) The illustrator painted at a quiet pace, pausing to light his pipe, and oblivious to the sounds of the children nearby.

Mary Rockwell's letters, reproduced in the Appendix of this book, are evidence of the deep bond that existed between her and Norman Rockwell. The letters also reveal her accomplishments as a writer. Having studied writing at Stanford University, Mary Rockwell maintained her interest in writing throughout her life, although she never published any work other than an occasional article which she wrote in her husband's name. Her admiration of fine literature extended into the field of children's books and she gathered an extensive collection over the years. Ann Marsh remembered Mary Rockwell's activity in the community, having served with her on the library board, and recalled her involvement in an intense community controversy over the use of school buses to transport the high school basketball team.

While Mary pursued her own interests, she also ministered to the psychological and practical needs of her husband. In addition to the many hours of reading to him, she attended to the multiple details supporting his work, making arrangements for props, screening phone calls and unwanted visitors, and shopping for food and incidentals. An intercom buzzer system was connected between the studio and the house, the number of buzzes signifying

All of Rockwell's studios were constructed according to a similar design. The studio in West Arlington—in which the illustrator is shown selecting photographs for an illustration—was not very different from his earlier studio down the road or his later studio in Stockbridge.

ABOVE: *After the Honeymoon.* Original oil painting for a *Saturday Evening Post* cover, August 23, 1930.

BELOW: *The Common Cold.*

There were certain dangers in Rockwell family members posing for the illustrator. After appearing on the *Post* as a neglected wife shortly after her marriage to Norman Rockwell, Mary Rockwell received a sympathetic letter from a friend in California who drew inaccurate conclusions about the status of the Rockwell marriage. More true to life perhaps was the scene of the common cold, shown below, in which Mary Rockwell ministers to her son Peter.

the message being transmitted. The phone in the studio could be turned off, so that Mary could answer without disturbing her husband; then she would buzz the studio if the call required his attention. Only visitors known to the Rockwells were permitted to saunter into the studio unannounced. In fact, Marie Briggs, one of the Rockwell cooks, refused to admit Rockwell's friend, Walt Disney, until his entrance was announced on the intercom in advance. The most frequent signal on the intercom was usually directed to Mary Rockwell: "Come out and look at the picture," which she did at a moment's notice. She was his most intelligent critic.

The three Rockwell sons were born in New Rochelle—Jarvis in 1931, Tom in 1933, and Peter in 1936. Once in Arlington they attended the local schools. For a while, Jarvis and Tom attended Oakwood, a boarding school in Poughkeepsie recommended by the family friend Dorothy Canfield Fisher, and Peter went to Putney. (Two of the three boys eventually married girls they had met at boarding school.)

The eldest, Jarvis Rockwell—Jerry, as he was called as a boy—was eight years old when the family moved to Arlington. He did not welcome the move, having already formed his early attachments in New Rochelle. From the casually accepted comforts of their home on Lord Kichener Road, the Rockwells took up residence in a secluded farmhouse on a back road in Arlington where the screeching of bobcats seemed a nightly reminder of their isolation. The community continued to drag the weight of the Depression years at its heels. Many neighbors were still on the welfare rolls, and there was the shock of seeing a boy come barefoot to class in the middle of the winter.

Jarvis Rockwell did not take easily to the shift. He never altogether overcame the sense of having been transplanted. Although the Rockwells were well received, they were not natives, and the subtle distance that separated them from the Vermonters seemed to be more disconcerting to the eldest son than to the others. Because fitting in did not come easily to the introspective Jerry, he tended to remove himself from the others, "lying in a hammock all summer," he said. While he showed talent for drawing, he refused to consider any form of commercial art, a natural result, no doubt, of having such a renowned illustrator in the family. Quite abruptly, in the middle of his senior year, Jarvis dropped out of high school to study art at the Art Students League and at the National Academy of Design in New York City. Rockwell encouraged his son in this pursuit, transforming a corncrib into a studio for him behind the house and supporting him financially for years. Jarvis Rockwell is still a fine artist ("totally incapable of being commercial," he has said), and working in an approach his father would call "very modern."

When he was a child, Jarvis posed for his father only a few times, "probably because I wasn't the type of cute kid he wanted for his pictures." After Jarvis passed through his awkward adolescent years, Rockwell tended

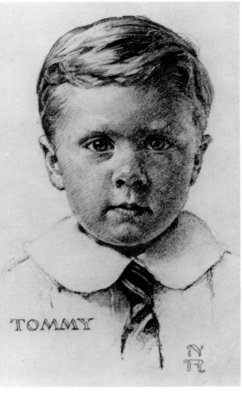
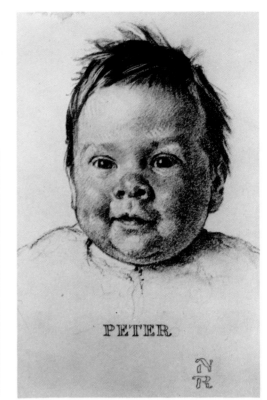

Jerry. Private Collection.　　*Tommy.* Private Collection.　　*Peter.* Private Collection.

to use him more frequently, and he appeared in one of the illustrator's most popular illustrations, *Saying Grace*, just before he enlisted in the Air Force at the age of nineteen.

Quite unlike Jarvis, the middle son Tommy was determined to fit into his environment. He was popular with his classmates, played on the school's basketball team, was yearbook editor and valedictorian. He was extremely attached to the Edgertons, and was just as likely to be in their home as his own. Tom posed fairly often for his father, the ideal Cub Scout to Buddy Edgerton's Boy Scout, and was the most athletic of the Rockwell men. He was responsible for convincing his father to construct the tennis court in the back of the house.

The closest Tom came to taking an interest in art was when he studied photography, a brief pursuit that was replaced by a more intense commitment to writing poetry. (He is now an author of children's books, including the very popular, *How to Eat Fried Worms*.) In the late 1950s Rockwell was approached with the idea of publishing his autobiography. The ghost writer originally sent by the publisher was intent on creating a Horatio Alger tale—from rags to riches—an approach Rockwell found laughable. Instead, Rockwell suggested his son for the job—the young man was a magazine editor by then—and Tom Rockwell did an admirable job of transforming his father's recollections into an entertaining manuscript called *My Adventures as an Illustrator*.

Like Jarvis, Peter Rockwell also decided to become an artist. Unlike his older brother, however, Peter was already in his last year at Haverford College when he announced his decision. His father was dismayed. "He'd lost his last opportunity to have one solid professional in the family," Peter

Graduation. Original oil painting for a
Saturday Evening Post cover, June 6, 1959.

Throughout the years, Rockwell depicted his sons as they were growing up.
Jarvis appeared in a game of marbles for
the first *Post* cover Rockwell painted
in Arlington, and Tommy's graduation
from college prompted his father to paint
the 1959 cover for the *Post*.

Playing Marbles. Saturday Evening Post cover,
September 7, 1939.

laughed. "And the only thing worse than being a painter or poet was being
a sculptor." Norman Rockwell resisted it over a year, finally giving in only
after consulting his friend Erik Erikson, the distinguished psychoanalyst.
Peter Rockwell eventually became a sculptor, and settled in Rome, Italy, in
an environment where the staggering artistic heritage may have helped
place the impressive achievements of his father in greater perspective.

While being the offspring of a father totally dedicated to his work may
not always have been easy, Rockwell was by no means an unkind parent. If
his involvement with work occupied most of his waking energies, he did
not insist on imposing single-mindedness on his sons by confining their
behavior to accommodate his patterns. Unlike many artists, Rockwell
permitted the children to wander in and out of the studio freely, enjoying
the sound of their laughter and the flurry of activity they brought with
them. Peter Rockwell remembers going into the studio quite regularly to
read. And all the children recall the richness of Halloween costumes they
found in their father's treasure trove of items used for his pictures. For all his
set ways, Rockwell was not a stern father. "After all," said the youngest
Rockwell, "Pop was forty-two when I was born. By that time your habits are
fixed." Rockwell may have been preoccupied, but he was not authoritarian.
For example, there was the time the family went to California for a few
months, living in a hotel at the end of Hollywood Drive in a neighborhood
where ten movie theaters were situated within an eight-block radius. Then
twelve years old, Peter Rockwell, who had been growing up in a town
where the nearest movie house was eight miles away, was determined to
taste the pleasures of every film in the area. He managed to see nine double
features in a seven-day period.

There wasn't much time for holidays, but occasionally Rockwell would
take his sons from Vermont into New York for three or four days—a great
adventure—to attend the circus or drive down to the Bowery early in the
morning. Peter Rockwell remembers when they went to Rockefeller Center
one morning so early that the escalators hadn't yet been turned on.
"Running up and down those stationary escalators was one of the great
moments of my life. It was magical," he recalls. Without being too permis-
sive, therefore, the Rockwell parents did allow their children the freedom
of discovery.

Norman Rockwell drew on the events in the family as inspiration for his
work, and incorporated his three boys and wife into many of his pictures. In
later years, after Mary's death and after the children were grown, he went
farther afield for subject matter and for models. The paintings that follow,
therefore, are a family album that chronicles the Rockwell family in
Arlington, Vermont. Among this group is some of his best work.

This is a genuine family reunion, bringing together all the Rockwells in a single painting. At the left edge of the painting is Peter Rockwell, who recently referred to himself as "the fat kid with glasses," recalling this as a particularly nasty period of his adolescence. In the plaid shirt Tom Rockwell is standing with his hands in his pockets, while Mary Rockwell embraces her son Jarvis and Norman Rockwell—pipe between his lips—looks on affectionately. The idea for the cover was inspired by Jarvis' homecoming from Oakwood, although the actual event never occurred. "We weren't a family given to that kind of display," said Peter Rockwell. Had such an occasion actually taken place, however, the same members of the group might just as well have assembled for such a homecoming. The three smiling girls in the center of the last row are, from left to right, Patty Schaeffer, Mary Atherton, and Lee Schaeffer. Mead Schaeffer stands behind Peter Rockwell and behind Grandma Moses, the painter, who was a friend of the Rockwells living in a nearby town. On the other side of the painting, standing behind Norman Rockwell, is Ann Marsh, with her baby Donny, and Mary Immen Hall. The boy in the foreground is Don's brother, Chuck Marsh, who posed for *Day in a Boy's Life*. The twin girls are actually one Sharon O'Neil, the daughter of Arlington's Dr. O'Neil. When Sharon came to pose for Rockwell, she wore a charming plaid skirt. After painting the plaid in Tommy's shirt and the patterns on the packages, however, Rockwell felt any more plaids would be too distracting. Ann Marsh recalled that Rockwell took the trouble to phone the O'Neil parents to be sure they didn't object to his making the skirt red in the painting. "That was so typical of his thoughtfulness," Mrs. Marsh observed. "As if anyone would mind!"

1. Sharon O'Neil
2. Grandma Moses
3. Peter Rockwell
4. Mead Schaeffer
5. Rena Crofut
6. Tom Rockwell
7. Patty Schaeffer
8. Mary Rockwell
9. Mary Atherton
10. Jarvis Rockwell
11. Lee Schaeffer
12. Norman Rockwell
13. Ann Marsh
14. Donny Marsh
15. Mary Immen Hall
16. Sharon O'Neil
17. Chuck Marsh

Family Homecoming. Original oil painting for a *Saturday Evening Post* cover, December 25, 1948. Old Corner House Collection, Stockbridge, Massachusetts.

Storyteller or *Benedict's Garage*. Original oil painting for a *Saturday Evening Post* cover, October 13, 1945. Collection Judy and Alan Goffman. Courtesy Phillips Fine Art Auctioneers, New York.

arvis and Peter Rockwell both posed for this *Post* cover, a painting Norman Rockwell felt was successful because of its authenticity. "Everyone was real," he said. Peter Rockwell has faint memories of this wonderful, dark, greasy garage. "I think Pop actually *added* light to it for the painting," he laughed. The group surrounding the storyteller could have been as real as the interior of the garage itself. John Benedict, who built cabinets and stairs for Norman Rockwell and delivered mail to him during the war, sits on the table alongside the real owner of the garage, his brother Bob Benedict, Jr. Hefty Nip Noyes, and lean Herb Squires are seated at the right. Duane Peters, a former marine discovered by Norman Rockwell at a Grange Hall square dance, posed for the storyteller.

Benedict's Garage was somewhat of a hangout in Arlington, but no place was finer for a gathering than the family's rustic camping lodge in Benedict's Hollow up the mountain. (Dr. Russell had a camp of his own just below the Benedicts'.) The Rockwell boys enjoyed going there, and Rockwell himself, though he wasn't much of a card player, would join in for the "clam feeds" prepared by the neighbors. A black bear caught in the wilds in 1943 was occasion enough for a grand party at the camp. 🦅

Jarvis Rockwell had just enlisted in the U.S. Air Force when he posed for his father in *Saying Grace*. He remembers that the painting did not come easily. George Hughes also remembers the difficulty Rockwell had with it. According to Hughes, Rockwell threw the canvas into the snow one night, so discouraged had he become, but returned to it the next day, determined to make it work. Given all the trouble he had with it, Rockwell never imagined it would become one of his most popular covers.

Rockwell went to the railroad diner in Troy, New York, more than once to get the qualities of light and the details for the setting. Just how to paint a railroad yard on a winter afternoon through a rain-soaked window was a challenge the artist couldn't resist, in spite of the complexity of these technical problems. Tables and chairs were shipped to Rockwell's studio from an automat in New York City. ("A truck pulled up, deposited the furniture, then took it away a few days later," recalled the cook, Marie Briggs.) And every detail was selected, examined, and placed carefully in the painting: the mugs of coffee, the suitcase, knitting bag, umbrellas, and cigarettes supporting the story in the painting and collectively forming a tight composition at the same time. "My father was very different from most other twentieth-century artists. He was a thinking painter rather than a visual painter," observed Peter Rockwell who is an artist and art historian himself. "There are no useless details in this painting, and every detail has a design function as well. For example, even the red seats on the chairs have been used to isolate the figures in the center of the composition. Nothing is left to chance. Everything is exceptionally well thought out."

Rockwell's selection of Bill Sharkey for the figure on the left holding the umbrella was particularly astute. Sitting all day long on a wooden chair at the edge of his porch, Sharkey was a self-styled derelict who seemed to enjoy doing as little as possible. Rockwell figured Sharkey would be a type likely to frequent a railroad diner such as this. (A good friend of Sharkey's, another local character named Hoddy Woodard, would also have been suitable, but his practice of wearing the same outfit for six months in succession made the odor too unbearable for an indoor photo session, Rockwell maintained.) Others in the painting include Don Winslow at the table with the elderly Mrs. Ralph Walker, who never lived to see the painting published. At the table in the foreground is Rockwell's assistant Gene Pelham. 🍎

Saying Grace. Original oil painting for a *Saturday Evening Post* cover, November 24, 1951. Collection Mr. and Mrs. Ken Stuart.

I wasn't the cute type," Jarvis Rockwell remarked, which explains why Rockwell rarely painted his oldest son in boyhood. Rockwell painted Jarvis as a young man instead. After returning from service in the Air Force, Jarvis continued to study art seriously, a fact that inspired Norman Rockwell to paint *The Critic*. This subject gave the illustrator the opportunity to play with his favorite Old Masters, the sixteenth-century Dutch and Flemish painters. Indebted to them for his palette and technique, Rockwell enjoyed making these satirical renditions of works of Frans Hals and Peter Paul Rubens, an idea made even more amusing to him when his wife Mary posed for the Rubens portrait. The concept was easier than the execution. Rockwell must have made fourteen or fifteen sketches before he came up with the appropriately comical expression. 🍎

The Critic. Original oil painting for a *Saturday Evening Post* cover, April 16, 1955. Old Corner House Collection, Stockbridge, Massachusetts.

The Pocket Game. Saturday Evening Post cover, January 25, 1936.

Boy Reading Sister's Diary. Saturday Evening Post cover, March 21, 1942.

Tommy Rockwell was three years old when he posed for the child searching through his great Uncle Gil's pocket to find a present, and he was nine when he posed for the boy reading his sister's diary. Posing for the second cover, he grew restless in the uncomfortable seat placed in front of his mother's dressing table. Rockwell reported that he had to bribe his son to keep him still for the photographs. Tommy was also a good subject for Rockwell's Boy Scout calendars. These calendars could become tedious for the illustrator, and many times he considered giving them up entirely. The subject was limited at best, particularly because no humor was permitted. If a minor error was made in the color, insignia, or details of the uniform, the painting was returned for correction. Begun originally on a voluntary basis, the annual calendars became so profitable that Rockwell couldn't afford *not* to paint them, especially during the long months, without pay, when he would work on a single *Post* cover to get it just right. (He also felt a certain loyalty, having painted the calendars for so many years.) Determined to achieve accuracy in the Boy Scout pieces, Rockwell painted an authentic but intimate detail in the 1946 calendar: the unmistakable expression of concentration evident around Tommy's mouth. He and brother Peter teamed up for the 1948 calendar, in which the younger boy played the Cub Scout and Tommy posed for one of the hiking figures. As a young man, Tommy posed for the 1953 calendar.

On My Honor. Original oil painting for Boy Scout poster-calendar. © 1953 Brown & Bigelow, Inc., a Division of Saxon Industries, Inc.
Collection Boy Scouts of America.

Boy on a Diving Board. Original oil painting for a *Saturday Evening Post* cover, August 16, 1947. Courtesy Martin Diamond Fine Arts, New York.

Men of Tomorrow. Original oil painting for Boy Scout poster-calendar. © 1948 Brown & Bigelow, Inc., a Division of Saxon Industries, Inc. Collection Boy Scouts of America.

When Buddy Edgerton outgrew his role as Boy Scout, he was replaced by Freeman Grout of Arlington; when Tom Rockwell outgrew his role, he was replaced by his younger brother Peter. As a pair, Peter Rockwell and Freeman Grout posed for the 1949 and 1950 Scout calendars. These were minor events in Peter Rockwell's memory. Much more vivid is his recollection of posing as the boy on the diving board for the *Post* cover, August 16, 1947.

To prepare for the scene, Norman Rockwell wheeled his studio easel toward the steps of his balcony, then cranked up the easel to the highest point on its stand. He then placed a plank with one end resting on a step and the other on the top of the easel. The board was well above eye level, precisely the angle he wanted for the picture. So he hoisted his son onto the plank, quite delighted with himself. Peter was truly terrified as he peered down from those heights, giving Rockwell just the authenticity he wanted for the picture. Although the illustrator achieved the frightened expression he was after, he was less satisfied with the qualities of light. "It would have been much better," he said, "if I had posed the boy on the actual springboard instead of posing him in my studio as I did. You just can't simulate the effect of real sunlight." Peter Rockwell had little to say about the lighting in the painting. His mind was on other things. 🍎

Our Heritage. Original oil painting for Boy Scout poster-calendar. © 1950 Brown & Bigelow, Inc., a Division of Saxon Industries, Inc. Collection Boy Scouts of America.

Friend in Need. Original oil painting for Boy Scout poster-calendar. © 1949 Brown & Bigelow, Inc., a Division of Saxon Industries, Inc. Collection Boy Scouts of America.

To prepare a winter *Post* cover, Rockwell would have to work through the summer, undeterred by practical matters concerning physical comfort. Posing for this cover during the month of August was not one of Peter Rockwell's easiest assignments, but it turned out to be his most lucrative. Some preliminary photographs were taken in the studio, but to get it right Rockwell had to photograph the scene inside a dining car. Since bringing such a car into the studio seemed unfeasible, Rockwell decided to do the next best thing: he arranged for a dining car to be sidetracked at the New York Central train yards in New York City. It happened to be the hottest day in August when the crew drove down from Arlington to New York City for the photo session. Rockwell selected one of many waiters offered to him by New York Central and for two-and-a-half hours his models posed in winter clothing inside a dining car that was baking in the summer afternoon's heat. "I began to gripe," Peter remembered. "But Pop said if I just did it without complaining he would take me to F.A.O. Schwarz and buy me anything I wanted. I can still remember my triumph as we drove back to Vermont with my fabulous new toy truck in my lap. I was convinced I got the better end of the deal!" 🍎

Oil sketch for *Boy in Dining Car*. Courtesy Martin Diamond Fine Arts, New York.

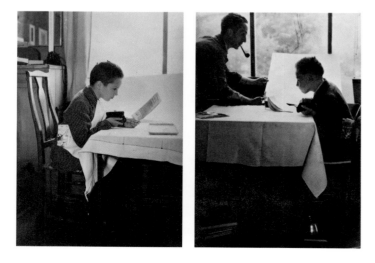

Boy in Dining Car. Original oil painting for a *Saturday Evening Post* cover, July 7, 1946. Private Collection, Old Corner House, Stockbridge, Massachusetts.

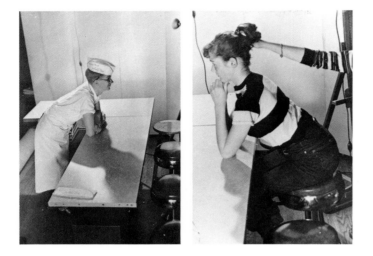

Norman Rockwell was living in Stockbridge and Peter Rockwell was a junior at Putney, a boarding school in Vermont, when his father decided to paint this cover for the *Post* in 1953. Rockwell came to the idea from talking to Peter who had had a summer job as a soda jerk at a local establishment the previous summer. It seemed most appropriate, therefore, that Peter pose for the cover, so the illustrator drove up to Putney and charmed the headmistress into allowing his son to return to Stockbridge with him for the weekend, along with eight or ten other classmates. Among the students who came to pose for the picture was Cynthia Ide, Peter's future wife. It is a little known fact that she posed for this painting, probably because only a part of her figure (the rear part, in fact) was used for the painting. As long as he had his models for the appointed sessions, Rockwell was a benevolent host for the bunch, leaving them free to do as they pleased during their visit. It turned out to be a weekend of parties, a coincidental but fitting send-off to Peter's last cover for Norman Rockwell. 🍎

Soda Jerk. Saturday Evening Post cover, August 22, 1953.

Stockbridge

CELEBRATION AND MOURNING

Main Street, Stockbridge, at Christmas. Original oil painting for *McCall's* magazine, December, 1967. Old Corner House Collection, Stockbridge, Massachusetts.

The buildings along Stockbridge's Main Street are Rockwell landmarks. The Christmas tree is displayed in a large window Rockwell installed when he rented this space for his studio. The central red brick building was the location of the town clerk's office, where Rockwell's *Marriage License* was portrayed. The Red Lion Inn, closed during the winters until 1969, stands desolate on the right. At the very extreme right is seen Rockwell's white house and red studio.

T o the citizens of Stockbridge, the arrival of a celebrity was not an unusual addition to the community. The town had attracted men and women of distinction from the time its first missionary, John Sergeant, had settled there in 1734. It was in Stockbridge that this industrious minister transformed a depleted tribe of Mahican Indians into Americanized colonists. Until they were nudged out gradually by ambitious settlers in later years, the tribe represented a unique group, the only Indians to assume an American name—the Stockbridge Indians—for their tribe and to fight on the side of the colonists in the Revolutionary War.

Others were equally drawn to Stockbridge for the promise of an improved life. Up the Housatonic River from Connecticut came settlers who prospered from the mills made productive by the great source of local water power. Over the years, Stockbridge has attracted a varied group of cultured and well-to-do families from Connecticut, New York, and Boston. Just as tolerance of the Indians made the town unique in the eighteenth century, acceptance of eccentricity continues today. "The town is prosperous, but not commercial," offered Walter Scott, a photographer from San Francisco who has lived next door to the Rockwells since 1961. "Except for the wealth brought by successful professionals and summer people, the town has little economic basis for its prosperity today. Its foundation has always been philosophical rather than commercial."

Scott's point of view is supported by the numbers of cultured individuals who came to Stockbridge. Writers Nathaniel Hawthorne, Henry Wadsworth Longfellow, and Herman Melville settled there. Tanglewood, the summer outdoor music festival, was created in Stockbridge. The Berkshire Theatre has brought to Stockbridge the most prominent performers of the day, and Daniel Chester French—the sculptor who created the statue of Abraham Lincoln for the memorial in Washington, D.C.—lived there. In his treatment facility located in the center of town, Dr. Austen Riggs achieved remarkable results with the mentally ill. Reinhold Niebuhr, the theological philosopher, Erik H. Erikson, the psychoanalyst and writer, as well as photographers, philosophers, writers, musicians, actors, celebrities seeking a retreat: all continue to live side by side in privacy, in Stockbridge, Massachusetts, a community whose entire population during the winter is not more than 2,200.

The Rockwells' move to Stockbridge in 1953 did not create a stir. Mary Rockwell's continued treatment at the Austen Riggs Foundation was hardly considered out of the ordinary. So many people before and since (and so many of them famous) had come to Stockbridge for the same reason. And Rockwell used Riggs' patients as models and photographers. Nor were Rockwell's connections with publishing and advertising particularly unusual. Though he certainly was among the most prominent members of this circle, he was not alone. New York writers and publishers had been living in Stockbridge for years. It was almost as if Rockwell had returned halfway to New Rochelle; although Stockbridge was certainly not a New York City suburb, it was less rural than Arlington had been. New friends and new models stimulated him, and the *Post* covers he created during his first years in Stockbridge are among his finest.

If the early years in his new home proved productive, they also represented a difficult time for him. Mary Rockwell showed only minimal improvement, though she had taken to drawing and was working with David Loveless at the Riggs workshop. ("She had talent, too," her instructor recalled.) The house was silent now: Peter and Tom Rockwell were off at school; Jarvis lived elsewhere. And Norman Rockwell was older, suffering from occasional back pains and preoccupied with his wife's illness. Even his work was troubling him. He had experienced periods of self-doubt before, but the fear of losing his touch seemed particularly acute during this time. He confided in Erik Erikson his apprehensions and he assiduously worked to improve his painting. On Tuesday mornings he attended a life drawing class at Peggy Best's studio. The fast sketches he turned out during these two-and-a-half

Landscape Painting. Estate of Norman Rockwell.

In later years Rockwell kept himself "loosened up" with rapid oil sketches. These impasto landscape paintings represented a departure from his earlier subjects and techniques.

hour sessions loosened him up. His work nourished him, renewed him, and to those who saw him every day he appeared to be in good cheer and enthusiastic about his latest painting.

But the Rockwells' life in Stockbridge was very different now. Not that Rockwell felt any regrets. (He was as unlikely to look back on his life as he was to look back on a painting he'd finished. Only the next painting interested him.) It was simply a different town and a different time. The town was larger and more cosmopolitan than Arlington, and without young children in the home, the Rockwells were less connected to the community. Rockwell's recent assignments required travel, and when they were in town, their social life tended to be with the family itself. The boys—by now young men—returned for holidays and were soon bringing home wives to entertain as well. No circle of artists replaced the great fellowship shared with the Schaeffers, the Athertons, and the Hugheses.

Except for Chris Schafer, who came down from Vermont twice a week to attend to the books, the Rockwells rarely saw their Arlington friends. Instead, a new circle developed to replace them. Rockwell and Harry Dwight, the president of the bank in Stockbridge, formed an informal group of peers which they called The Marching and Chowder Club. The charter members consisted of six or eight gentlemen and a number of occasional visitors, including psychoanalyst Erikson, playwright Thornton Wilder, and critic Walter Prichard Eaton. Each Thursday these gentlemen convened for lunch to exchange tall stories and philosophical thoughts.

When they came to Stockbridge, the Rockwells first lived on West Main Street, directly across the street from the town physician, Dr. Donald Campbell. Mary Rockwell would come to chat with Dr. Campbell almost every morning and enjoyed spending time with his daughter Betsy, suggesting perhaps that she missed the companionship of a young child.

For studio space, Norman Rockwell rented two rooms over the meat market on Main Street, replacing the small double-hung windows facing north with a single large studio window. He worked there until they moved into a colonial house on South Street across from the Red Lion Inn in 1957. At the back of his home Rockwell had Ejner Handberg remodel an old carriage house for him, converting it into a studio that looked very much like the one he'd loved in Arlington.

The Rockwells were within walking distance of the shops, restaurants, post office, and town folk. Norman Rockwell became a familiar sight to the neighbors as he'd nod hello (without stopping to chat) on his way down the street to purchase a newspaper or a packet of tobacco. An eager mother might discreetly parade her child before him in the hope that the illustrator would offer an invitation for the child to pose for him. (Not unrealistic: Rockwell selected more than one model from such "chance" encounters.)

Through the 1950s and into the early 1960s Rockwell maintained the pace of a young man, despite his advancing age. By simplifying his working methods, he was able to accomplish more within a shorter period of time. In earlier years he photographed details in isolation from one another: one model, then the other; one prop, then another. Only when absolutely necessary did he take his photographer on location to shoot. He preferred to have what he needed delivered to the studio. For a given painting, a horse, pullman seat, chicken, or piano might arrive at the studio door. After the details were photographed, Rockwell assembled them to fit his concept. In later years, however, Rockwell was likely to arrange more of the composition at a single session. He might take his photographer on location—to a local luncheonette or to the town clerk's office— and photograph all the models in place at the same session, composing his painting and photograph simultaneously, working with fewer pictorial fragments.

Rockwell was less connected personally to his models in later years than he was earlier in his career. He painted more celebrities now, public figures in politics, entertainment, and sports. Models also continued to be neighbors, of course, but rarely were they close friends. During the 1950s and into the 1960s he was no less particular about the specific requirements for a model, but he was not always acquainted with the person who came to the studio. Louie Lamone might take a Polaroid photo of a potential candidate, which Rockwell would approve. In the last years, Lamone remembered that the illustrator even became less fussy about specific choices.

For something very unusual, or when he worked in a strange city, Rockwell might turn to a modeling agency. For example, in 1955 he went down to New York with Peter Rockwell to locate a mermaid for a *Post* cover. No self-respecting young woman in Stockbridge would want to pose naked to the waist for this subject, so he consulted nude photographs sent from a modeling agency in the city, and chose a French model from a lineup of several attractive females paraded before him at the agency. "My father told me that when she posed, the photographer was so embarrassed he wouldn't come out from behind the camera. He just hid under the black cloth," remembered Peter Rockwell, who wasn't allowed in the studio for the session. "Even though Pop concealed the explicit details of her breasts by covering the nipples with the slats of a lobster cage, he still received irate letters from offended readers!"

Rockwell's uncanny knack for taking catnaps during the working day enabled him to extend his energies even further. No matter where he was working—in the studio or on location—Rockwell could stretch out on a bench or on the floor and fall off to sleep immediately. Fifteen or twenty minutes later he would awaken refreshed and ready to go again.

With such energy, Rockwell continued to work his photographers very hard. He was lighthearted and friendly, but demanding. In Stockbridge, Rockwell used as photographers Bill Scovill, Clem Kalischer, and Louie Lamone. He called on his neighbor Walter Scott occasionally for photo-

Catch of the Day. Saturday Evening Post cover, August 20, 1955.

Discretion dictated that Rockwell select a professional model from an agency to pose for the mermaid.

Picasso vs. Sargent. Illustration for *Look*, January 11, 1966.

A one-day trip to Chicago's Art Institute for this cover did not fatigue the elderly illustrator. In fact, the young photographer working with Rockwell was far more worn out by the day's work.

graphs as well. Rockwell was nearly seventy years old when Scott flew out to Chicago with him for a day's shooting at the Art Institute. With three catnaps taken during the day ("stretched out on a bench in the museum"), Rockwell was still fresh and alert at 3:00 when the session was over. "I couldn't say the same for myself," said the young man. "I was exhausted." Seeing that the session had ended earlier than expected, Rockwell urged Scott to pack up the photography gear quickly so that they could try for an earlier flight back to New York. Rockwell paid $50 to a cab driver for a hair-raising ride to the airport, and was very pleased to catch a plane one hour earlier than originally scheduled. "I don't know how he managed to keep up that pace. By the time we got back to Stockbridge that evening I could barely stand up, but he was still feeling peppy, and reminded me that he wanted to see proofs first thing in the morning."

Rockwell was by then considered the distinguished elder statesman of commercial art, an historic figure, the last remaining vestige of the venerable Golden Age of Illustration. The artist's career was now being presented in retrospect. In 1960 the *Post* celebrated its long association with Rockwell by publishing his autobiography, *My Adventures as an Illustrator*, and the hardcover edition was published by Doubleday shortly thereafter. Times had changed.

Since the end of World War II, illustration itself had been in decline. Most of the magazines were turning to photography instead. The art director became the visionary, assuming far greater importance on the publication's staff. In 1959 Rockwell observed the change in the role of the art director when he wrote,

> No longer were they [the art directors] non-entities, errand boys who toted the illustrations and covers from the artist to the editor and back again. They were art directors once again and they *directed* art. Gradually, however, they began to overdirect. They usurped the role of the artist. Nowadays many illustrators use the art director's ideas rather than their own. And illustrators who are given ideas won't do as good work; they won't *feel* the pictures they are painting; the pictures aren't part of themselves. . . . Illustration is at a low point now. Maybe it's because so many of the illustrators have surrendered their own dignity and possibilities.

During that period many magazines encountered reverses. By the late 1950s the *Saturday Evening Post* itself was in its greatest financial crisis.

When Rockwell began with the *Post* in 1916, George Horace Lorimer, an eccentric and fiercely independent gentleman, was the editor. ("It was his magazine and his alone," Rockwell had said.) Lorimer showed far greater brilliance in running the magazine than he did in selecting his successor when he retired in 1936. Only because of the magazine's intensely loyal readership—developed by Lorimer over the years—was the magazine able to withstand the editorial leadership of the ultra-conservative Wesley Stout. After six years with Stout the magazine began to stumble badly, rescued by Ben Hibbs, the soft-spoken and kindly man who became editor in 1942. ("Easy going and quiet, but with iron in his soul," said Rockwell.) Hibbs intensified the written coverage of the war, commissioned Mead Schaeffer to paint fourteen commemorative war covers, and published Rockwell's *Four Freedoms*. Like several other mass-circulation magazines, however, the *Post* did not adapt with sufficient flexibility and ingenuity to the post-War generation. While the company was reshaping old formulas, a new breed of publisher was emerging, innovators with magazines that had more immediate appeal to the modern American reader: Harold Ross with *The New Yorker*; Henry Luce with *Fortune*, *Time*, and *Life*; DeWitt Wallace with *Reader's Digest*.

The *Post* was sliding. The simple folksiness did not seem relevant at a time when Fidel Castro was waging his revolution and the Civil Rights struggle made headlines. In 1961, the first year in its history that the Curtis Publishing Company operated at a loss, Hibbs resigned from the *Post*, and a totally revamped publication was announced with an appropriate cover by Norman Rockwell. The eight covers by Rockwell that followed illustrate the dubious course the magazine maintained for its survival. In an attempt at greater immediacy, the *Post* commissioned Rockwell to do portraits of international celebrities. Although these and his presidential candidates are excellent portraits (and Rockwell enjoyed doing them), they signaled the end of the *Post*'s eagerness to employ Rockwell for his narrative capabilities. His long tenure with the publication was terminated in 1963.

Rockwell made this drawing of himself and his wife Molly for a personal Christmas card, 1967.

It would be difficult to assess precisely to what extent leaving the *Post* affected his work. He was never short of assignments. (On the contrary, he had too many, and encountered difficulties keeping up with all his commissions.) Without the *Post*, however, Rockwell was disoriented, for no publication could give him the artistic freedom he had enjoyed for forty-seven years. The covers for the *Post* had represented a unique arena for Norman Rockwell and such an opportunity would never again be available to him—or to any other illustrator. Magazine covers were now more restricted in function, now designed to attract readers with the immediacy of their message. Tied to the contents of the specific issues of the magazines, these covers attracted the busy readers with an image that suggested urgency. The covers for the *Post*—and the strength of Rockwell's contribution to that publication—projected situations that were independent of the specific contents of the issue itself. The images mirrored the yearnings of the readership and described the magazine by reflecting a profile of its readers. They were self-contained images that projected the aspirations inherent in the American dream, and Rockwell was the greatest of these mythic creators. Magazines no longer reached families who lingered over their contents in the same way. Magazine covers now competed with one

Redesigning the Post Cover. Saturday Evening Post cover, September 16, 1961. Old Corner House Collection, Stockbridge, Massachusetts.

another to win readers away from the more appealing medium of television.

Without the *Post*, Rockwell now had new relationships to establish, new kinds of demands that could not have come easily to the seventy-year-old illustrator. Even so, he happily accepted assignments from *Look* and *McCall's*, and took off into entirely new directions as a result.

If the changing trends in magazine publishing disappointed him, other changing fashions were even more disturbing. Illustrators, regarded as popular heroes until World War II, had declined in influence after the War. By the 1950s the American cultural heroes being celebrated were the Abstract Expressionists. Illustrators were considered "low brow" by "high brow" standards. An article written by Wright Morris in the *Atlantic Monthly* was critical of Norman Rockwell for destroying the taste of the American people. For the first time in his career, Rockwell was placed on the defensive by the very medium of communication that had once exalted him. And it hurt.

The shock of Mary Rockwell's sudden death—a massive coronary that claimed her life during a mid-day nap in the summer of 1959—left Norman Rockwell griefstricken, and it was several months into 1960 before he experienced any release from his despair. At the persistent urging of his friends Rockwell made an effort to socialize, to take up outside interests.

It was this motive that propelled him to an adult education class on

On assignment for Pan American Airways, Rockwell traveled around the world. Throughout the last twenty years of his life, he traveled extensively, always stimulated by the sights, costumes, and customs, and particularly by the people he met everywhere.

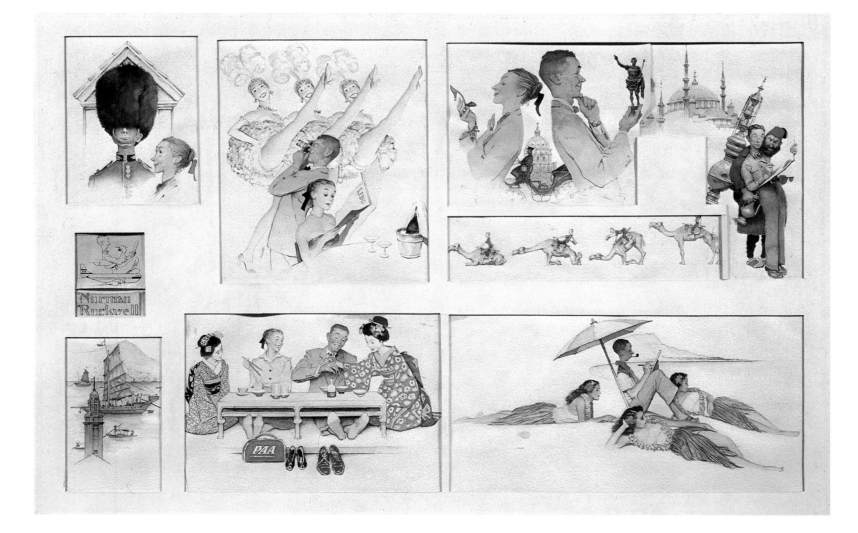

poetry at the Lenox, Massachusetts, Library. The informal discussion group was under the direction of Molly Punderson, an English teacher recently retired from Milton Academy. Until she became personally acquainted with Norman Rockwell, Molly Punderson had hardly known who he was. In fact, she had never seen the inside pages of the *Saturday Evening Post*, having developed a pattern of reading the more sophisticated periodicals, such as *Century*, *Foreign Affairs*, and *Atlantic*. Norman Rockwell? Until he moved to Stockbridge, she'd barely heard of him.

The poetry class may have been therapeutic for Rockwell, but he was not a serious student. "Norman was such a naughty boy at those sessions," Molly Rockwell recalled. "Our earnest discussions about Yeats and Eliot seemed to amuse him. Once, when we were interpreting the meaning of a poem by Robert Frost, in jest Norman offered to phone up the poet right then and there to ask what the poem meant. Why spend two hours talking about it when a phone call would settle it all?"

Molly Punderson and Norman Rockwell were married in 1961. "We wanted to dance in the street," remembered a Stockbridge neighbor. "We were so happy for Norman." Arlington friends were happy, too. Mary Schafer said, "Molly and Norman were well matched. They looked as if they'd known each other all their lives. They even resembled each other in an odd way."

Molly Punderson Rockwell is an independent and resourceful woman, qualities Norman Rockwell admired greatly. While she was sensitive to her husband's wishes, she did not neglect her own interests. After all, she'd been independent for sixty-four years and was not likely to change her ways entirely. For the first two years of their marriage, she maintained her old family house on Main Street. To escape tourists during the summer, Norman and Molly Rockwell ate dinner and breakfast and spent the night there until they decided to sell the house and consolidate their home in one location. Encouraged by Norman, she studied photography with her neighbor Walter Scott. "Considering that she had rarely picked up a camera before, it was remarkable how well she did with the equipment, as if she'd been working with it for years." Norman Rockwell painted from photographs she made while they traveled, using them primarily for background material. An old ice house on the Rockwell property was converted into a studio for her. Here she worked on the photography and wrote a book about a thrush called *Willie was Different*, which her husband illustrated.

Unlike Rockwell, Molly Punderson came from a rich New England heritage. On the paternal side of her family, Pundersons and Mellens date back to pre-Revolutionary days in New Haven and Berkshire. For Norman Rockwell, whose own parents had moved from one boardinghouse to another, Molly Rockwell provided a link to a past that placed him firmly within a Berkshire legacy.

Molly Rockwell gave Norman Rockwell a new lease on life. She was a

Portrait Sketch of a Russian Girl. Original painting. Old Corner House Collection, Stockbridge, Massachusetts.

During his travels to Russia, Rockwell painted a number of portraits, demonstrating this remarkable gift for a bold, painterly approach he had never exhibited before.

Springtime, Stockbridge. Original oil painting. Old Corner House Collection, Stockbridge, Massachusetts.

Riding his bicycle every day with his wife and friends, Rockwell became a familiar sight along the main roads of Stockbridge.

superb traveling companion. During the last decade of his active professional life, his assignments took them to different parts of the world, adventures they made with relish: to paint Nehru in India; Nasser in Egypt; the Peace Corps in Ethiopia; two trips to the Soviet Union; to Hollywood for the film "Stagecoach"; to Houston and Cape Canaveral for the launching of the astronauts. For vacations they went to Central America, the Caribbean, North Africa, the Riviera; and they frequently combined these trips with visits to Peter Rockwell who had settled with his family in Rome in the fall of 1961.

Rockwell's new assignments gave him the opportunity to paint more controversial subjects, political and social themes that were of current importance to the American public: desegregation of the schools, the Peace Corps, Civil Rights, the War on Poverty, the United Nations. No doubt Molly Rockwell contributed greatly to his sensibility in these areas, encouraging him to portray his humanitarianism in a format that would have the greatest impact on the American public. By contrast to these subjects, Rockwell also created more lyrical scenes, absent of any narrative whatsoever: Main Street, Stockbridge; portraits of Russian peasants; spring flowers. Now he was working in both horizontal and vertical formats, leaving behind the proportions dictated by the *Post* covers for so many years. His brushstrokes were freer; his colors bolder.

When he was in town, Rockwell continued to attend the weekly gatherings of The Marching and Chowder Club, though his favorite charter members had either moved or passed away, and he complained to Molly that the new group was not as "analythical" as the earlier one, an error in pronunciation she found too dear to correct. Molly and Norman Rockwell also joined the one-hundred-year-old Monday Evening Club, a group from

Pittsfield. On alternate Mondays a member would prepare a paper on a subject and read it aloud to the others. Rockwell was an excellent raconteur but found presenting a "subject" a formidable task. Under his direction, Molly Rockwell wrote on such topics as plagiarism in art and education in Russia, subjects the group found fascinating. On the evenings when it was the Rockwells' turn to entertain, dinner was ordered into the house from the Red Lion Inn and the group would adjourn afterwards to the studio, where the paper was read.

Such socializing became more infrequent with the years. Rockwell's age began to affect his pace. The town was becoming increasingly protective. It was not uncommon to see the elderly illustrator and his wife on their bicycles, riding through town and down Route 7. Accustomed to this sight, a driver would slow down and give the cyclists a wide berth. This was a measure of safety, but also a gesture of affection. "Seeing old Mr. Rockwell on his bike made you feel good," remembered Ed Locke. "You'd know he was feeling well and you wanted him to stay that way."

Rockwell's artistic powers were diminishing. Although he was still capable of turning out a superior painting during the mid-1960s, his work was uneven. He began to lose the delicacy of colors, a natural condition of age. Bright oranges and yellows, colors that had been unnatural to him, appeared in his work. "He didn't know they were getting garish," Peter Rockwell remembered. "I think his pictures would have held up anyway if he had only loosened up. But he tended to work against himself when he got nervous, and instead he would tighten up even more. When Molly would get him off on vacation he'd loosen up again. His paintings from these trips were free and impressionistic. But when he returned to the studio he'd fall into his old patterns and this would make him nervous again."

His weakening faculties did not diminish his appetite for work, however. What had been the center of his existence continued to spur him on with as much force as ever. He entered his studio every morning at the same time and took on new assignments, creating images for Franklin Mint's silver plates and commemorative medals. He created portraits of celebrities— Frank Sinatra, Arnold Palmer, John Wayne, Colonel Sanders—and he did more advertisements. Periodically he would become frustrated (or "nervous" as Peter Rockwell has described it) and would break away from the studio, taking a swiftly arranged trip with Molly.

On one trip to Holland Rockwell caught a cold and went to see a doctor. He was advised by the doctor to give up smoking his beloved pipe. Obediently, Rockwell threw away the pipe and stuck to the new regimen for about two weeks, suffering a great deal more from not smoking than he had from the cold. After returning to Stockbridge Rockwell consulted his physician, Dr. Paddock, who reassured his patient that it was acceptable for a man in his seventies to continue smoking his pipe. Rockwell was delighted, returning immediately to his pipe and his Edgeworth Executive Mixture.

The late 1960s brought a surge of renewed public interest in Rockwell, overshadowing any lingering fears the artist may have had of becoming a has-been. In 1969 Danenberg Galleries mounted the first solo exhibition of Rockwell's work. About fifty canvases were displayed in this fashionable New York gallery, a tribute to Rockwell's eminence as an illustrator whose original painting ranked with that of many of the most sought-after artists of the day.

Harry N. Abrams—the publisher of fine art books—also took Rockwell's work seriously by publishing the first major monograph on the illustrator in 1970. With text written by a museum director—Thomas Buechner—the book placed Rockwell within an historical context normally reserved for easel painters of the highest order. If Norman Rockwell was beloved until then, his stature as an artist rose to even greater heights with the publication of this handsomely produced book.

Norman Rockwell became a greater celebrity in the last years of his life than he had been during his sixty active years as an illustrator. Radio and television appearances were numerous. Museum exhibitions were held throughout the country: at the Museum of the Arts in Fort Lauderdale, at the Brooklyn Museum, at the Corcoran Gallery of Art in Washington, D.C., followed by traveling exhibitions in San Antonio, San Francisco, Oklahoma City, Indianapolis, Omaha, Seattle, and Philadelphia. Rockwell signed limited edition prints, created medals, and autographed books. The Old Corner House in Stockbridge displayed a permanent collection of Rockwell's most important works. In 1973 New Rochelle proudly staged a Norman Rockwell Day, a celebration that included renaming one of its streets Norman Rockwell Boulevard. That same year a documentary film was made on Rockwell, and a year later another film. In 1976 Stockbridge honored the illustrator with its own Norman Rockwell Day. A parade, floats, balloons, and music were all performed before the eighty-two-year-old illustrator who sat above the crowded streets on the reviewing stand.

These honors helped to offset Rockwell's frustrations with his work. Physically he was no longer able to create on canvas the images that still were alive in his imagination. Two bicycle accidents in 1974—the first at Little Dix in the Caribbean, the second in Stockbridge—had accelerated his physical deterioration, and work was increasingly difficult for him. A cover for *American Artist* in 1976—his last magazine cover—did not altogether meet his personal standards of excellence, and many other canvases remained unfinished because they failed to measure up under his scrutiny.

Even when he was no longer able to work at all, he made regular visits to his studio. It would be impossible to know what thoughts must have traveled through his mind as he sat silently in his chair, alone in the soft fading north light. His studio was his sanctuary to the end. When he died in 1978, an unfinished painting remained on his easel.

Happy Birthday. Bicentennial illustration.
© Billboard Publications, Inc.
Courtesy *American Artist* magazine.

Rockwell struggled with his painting for *American Artist*'s bicentennial issue, never altogether satisfied with the results. It was the artist's final magazine cover.

Patients and staff at the Austen Riggs Foundation, the psychiatric treatment facility in Stockbridge, provided a good source for Norman Rockwell's photographers and models. During the planning stages of *Marriage License* in the late winter of 1954, Rockwell asked a Riggs nurse to pose. She was unavailable, but suggested her sister Joan for the part. Sight unseen, Rockwell was pleased with this recommendation because Joan was about to be married and using a genuine couple for *Marriage License* appealed to him. He interviewed the young woman in his studio over the meat market and asked her to bring her fiancé, Moe, to him. "Knowing Moe as I do now," Joan Mahoney said recently, "I know he'd never have gone to be 'looked over' by some stranger. He must really have been in love with me then to do it!" Finding the pair ideal for his painting, Rockwell instructed them how to prepare for the photography session. Moe was to wear wing-tipped shoes and a pale blue (not white) shirt. Rockwell asked Joan to lighten her hair and to wear a bright yellow summer dress with puff sleeves. Finding a summer dress in the middle of the winter was not easy, particularly one so specific, and a dressmaker finally was called in to make it. By the time the Mahoneys posed for *Marriage License*, Rockwell had begun to consolidate his methods of assembling

reference material for his paintings. He photographed all three models at the same time and in the actual location of Stockbridge's town clerk's office. The models worked less than an hour, which was fortunate for Joan who was coming down with the flu and was chilly posing in a cotton dress in the middle of the winter. Rockwell instructed Moe Mahoney to squeeze his fiancée tightly ("Like you're in love with her," he directed), and she stretched onto her tiptoes as far as she could. While Bill Scovill photographed the two of them, Jason Braman, a shopkeeper who posed for the town clerk, waited his turn. Having lost his wife only recently, he was still feeling sad, and his son and daughter-in-law felt posing for Rockwell might cheer him up a bit. As he sat waiting his turn, he fell into this melancholy position and for the painting Rockwell eventually selected this accidental pose over the others.

Rockwell arrived at the initial figures almost immediately, but the color sketch shows the changes he made in the room's interior: he replaced the filing cabinets with a pot-bellied stove and made changes on the door. After the Mahoneys were married that May, Rockwell presented them with this oil sketch as a wedding gift, a characteristic gesture for the artist who never failed to demonstrate his gratitude toward his models. 🍎

Marriage License. Original oil painting for a *Saturday Evening Post* cover, June 11, 1955. Old Corner House Collection, Stockbridge, Massachusetts.

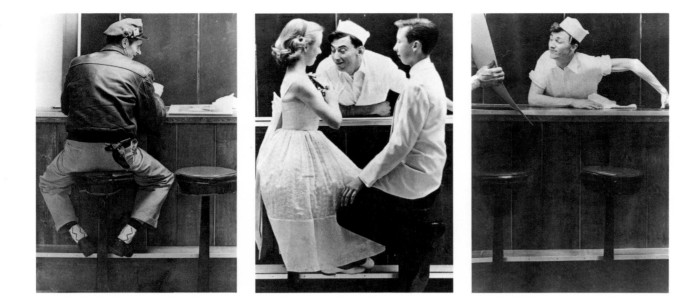

After posing his friend David Loveless for the soda
jerk in *After the Prom*, Norman Rockwell changed
his mind. The position of the arms was acceptable, but
Rockwell was looking for a different facial expression. So
he retained Loveless' arms and replaced the face with
that of his assistant Louie Lamone. (Lamone posed for
the figure at the left as well.) Artistically, *After the Prom*
is a curious combination of two Rockwell extremes: the
painting technique and subdued colors he adopted in
later years were in direct contrast to the element of
caricature pervasive in so much of his earlier work.
Rockwell himself was disappointed with the results. To
overcome what he perceived as a monotony of weak
chins, he concealed that part of the face on the left-hand
figure and used the girl's fingers to deemphasize the chin
on the soda jerk. But he was annoyed at himself because
he "was overcome by an irresistible impulse to caricature," as he confessed later. Rockwell varied the texture
here by mixing gravel with the pigment for effect, an
experiment that backfired: the paint surface eventually
crackled. ❦

After the Prom. Original oil painting for a *Saturday Evening Post* cover, May 25, 1957. Collection Mr. and Mrs. Thomas Rockwell.

The Campbells lived directly across the street from the Rockwells' first home in Stockbridge. Betsy, one of the four Campbell daughters, was a favorite of the neighbors, and as a youngster she frequently wandered over to pass the afternoon with Mary Rockwell. Riding down the street on a tricycle one day, Betsy Campbell was pursued by a dog yapping at her heels. Frightened, she lost her balance and took a nasty spill. Norman Rockwell, who happened to witness the accident, rushed to pick her up, brushed her off, and said reassuringly, "Don't worry about that. We'll fix it up right away." Holding her in his lap, he drew her a series of cartoons of a little girl riding a tricycle and being pursued by a dog. In the final picture the little girl is seen on the ground, her face licked all over by the dog, with a caption below saying, "You see, all he wanted to do was give you a kiss anyway." In recounting this event, Dr. Campbell cites this as typical of Rockwell's kindness, a simple gesture performed with love.

For the *Post* cover, the girl on the right, Anne Morgan, was selected because she was actually missing her front teeth. The illustrator asked Betsy Campbell to pose for the middle figure. Sewn by her mother, the plaid skirt Betsy wore was so charming that a letter to the *Post* from a reader in New York inquired about buying a half dozen of them. ❦

The Check-Up. Saturday Evening Post cover, September 7, 1957.

If Dr. Russell was the beloved family doctor in Arlington, Dr. Campbell could be considered Russell's counterpart in Stockbridge. Rockwell altered the interior of Dr. Campbell's office slightly, shifting the location of the furniture from one wall to another, but essentially maintaining the same elements in the room. In order to avoid taking too much of Dr. Campbell's time for posing, Rockwell had Louie Lamone pose for the body, then substituted the doctor's head at a later stage. Not so with the young man, however. Ed Locke was only about seven years old when he posed for this cover, and Rockwell

was so easy-going that the boy posed without shame, altogether unprepared for the effect it would have on his future reputation among his peers. After the cover appeared, his chums teased him mercilessly about the pose, and for years he heard that he'd sold his body for $5.00.

Other children in Stockbridge could look back on their modeling career with greater pride than Ed Locke might feel, however. Hank Bergmans, the child posing in the Boy Scout calendar, *Can't Wait!*, was thrilled when his picture was displayed everywhere. "It made me feel terrific," Bergmans remembered. 🐛

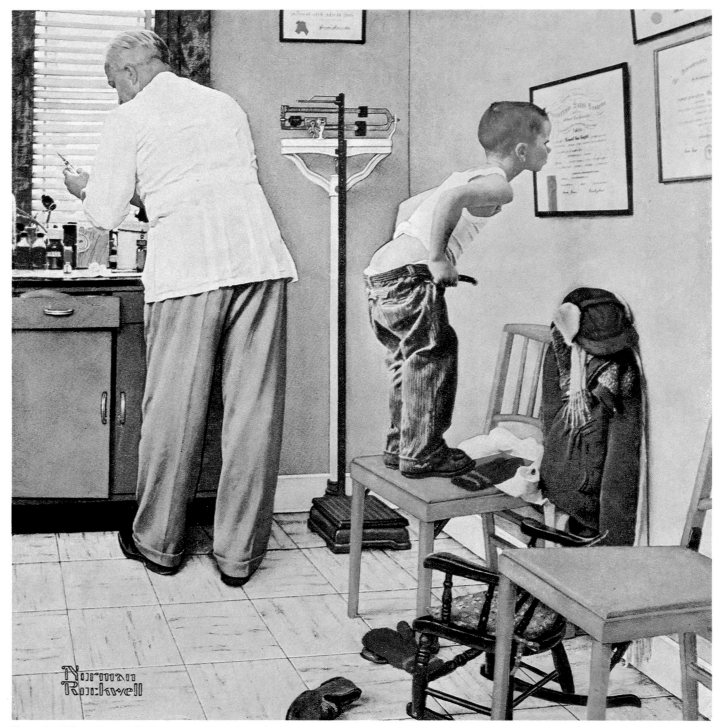

Doctor's Office. Original oil painting for a *Saturday Evening Post* cover, March 15, 1958. Collection Dr. and Mrs. Edward F. Babbott.

Can't Wait! Original oil painting for Boy Scout poster-calendar. © 1972 Brown & Bigelow, Inc., a Division of Saxon Industries, Inc. Collection Boy Scouts of America.

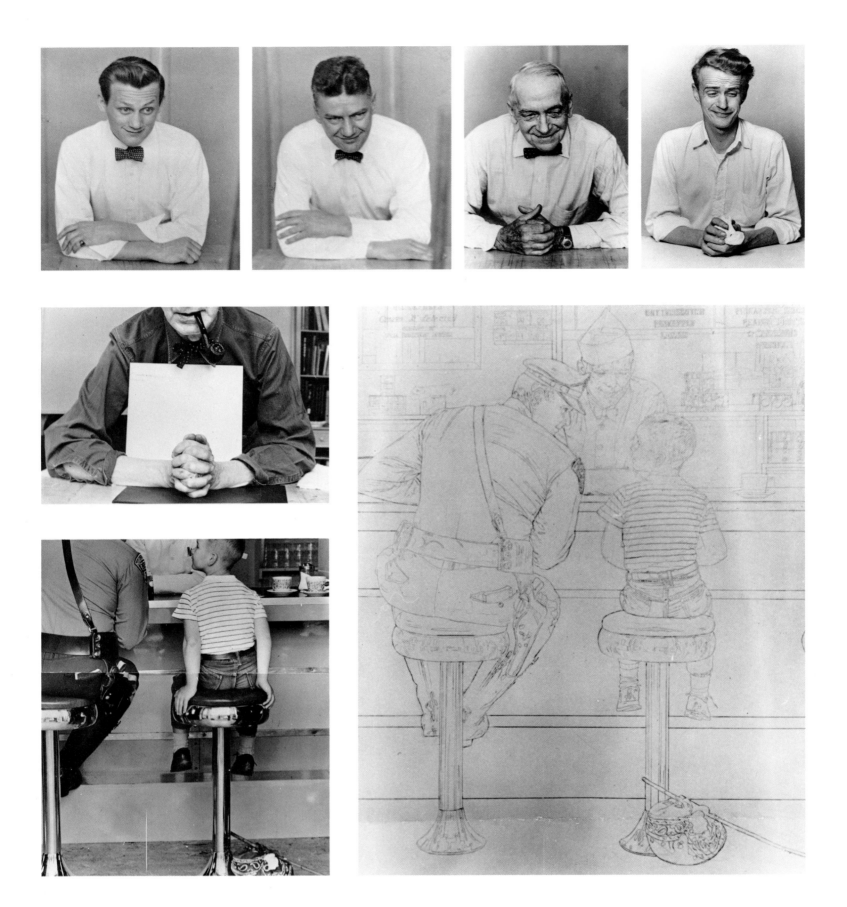

After posing for *The Doctor's Office*, Ed Locke was bound to be a bit more cautious the next time around, avoiding any assignments that might embarrass him again. Fortunately, *The Runaway* was harmless enough, and he even remembers having fun the day he posed for it at the Howard Johnson's in Pittsfield. There

he met Dick Clemens, a real state trooper, who was posing in the same picture. While the lunch counter scene was being prepared for photography, Clemens let Ed Locke sit inside his cruiser, showing him how to work the sirens and lights. "That was the most fun of all!" Locke remembered. Rockwell made several changes in

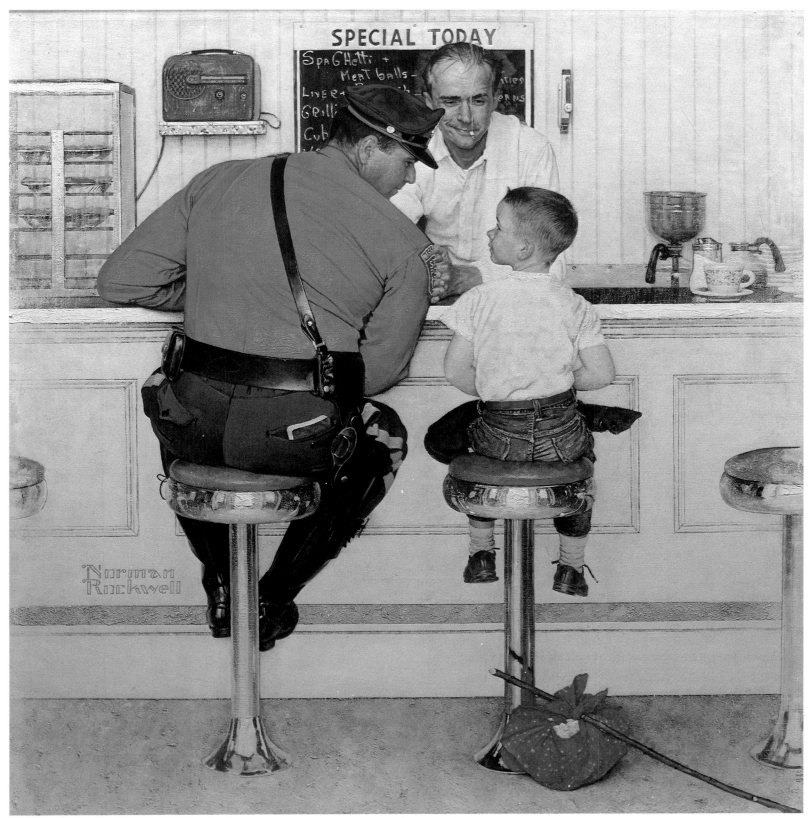

The Runaway. Original oil painting for a *Saturday Evening Post* cover, September 20, 1958. Old Corner House Collection, Stockbridge, Massachusetts.

the painting along the way, trying out many attendants until he found one with precisely the savvy expression he wanted. Rockwell had originally intended to use the Howard Johnson's interior for the final painting, but decided on a more rural-looking lunch counter in order to give the idea that the child had gone some distance before this event took place. 🍎

Tom Carey, the figure wearing black in *Elect Casey*, was the village character of Stockbridge. He was quite a horseman. Carey's business was transportation. Not exactly the big-time kind, but every day for about fifty years he transported the mail from the railroad station to the post office in his horse and buggy or sleigh. For additional income he would take tourists in his surrey on a rather informal tour through town. He was a great raconteur. Knowing the pedigree of everyone in Stockbridge, particularly the well-to-do, he would happily furnish some choice bits of gossip to spice up the tour a

bit. The town still refers to the time when he met Mrs. Austen Fox Riggs and offered her a ride home in his buggy. His spirited steed took off while he was lifting the "mooring stone," leaving Carey deposited by the side of the road. Mrs. Riggs was an excellent horsewoman, but Carey had put the reins where she couldn't reach them, and Mrs. Riggs held on for dear life until the horse reached his stable on Sergeant Street, where he stopped.

Tom Carey had many eccentricities, and everyone liked him, including Norman Rockwell. 🐦

Elect Casey. Original oil painting for a *Saturday Evening Post* cover, November 8, 1958. Collection *Saturday Evening Post*.

The Jury. Saturday Evening Post cover, February 14, 1959.

By the mid-1950s, Norman Rockwell had succeeded in simplifying his methods of developing a composition. Ten years before he might have photographed each of the eleven figures here individually, in his studio, combining them as a group with the interior in a composite drawing. Instead, he directed the scene with the eleven figures in place and on location. For the session, Rockwell asked his friend Oliver Kempton to gather some men in Stockbridge to pose for the jury, and in a single session Rockwell resolved the entire composition, adding the twelfth juror at the right and substituting himself for one of the standing figures. The members of the group include, from left to right: David Loveless, Norman Rockwell, Barbara Brooks, Louie Lamone (Rockwell's Man Friday), Byrne Bauer, Bill Obanheim, Ed Sullivan, Bob Williams, Bob Brooks (Barbara's husband), Oliver Kempton, Ken Hall, and Crandall. ❦

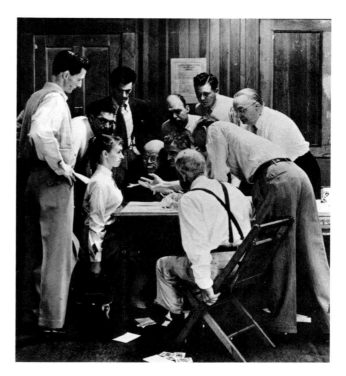

The Family Tree was the subject of frequent discussions between two generations of Rockwells. Peter Rockwell and his wife Cynthia urged Norman Rockwell to put a black man or woman at the bottom of the tree. The older Rockwell, seeing the validity of the idea, turned it around in his mind, but eventually decided the *Post* audience would not go for anything more provocative in the family than an Indian squaw and a swarthy pirate. "He was not a moralist," insisted Peter Rockwell. "He wanted to *please* his audience, not *challenge* it."

The family resemblance in the tree is not accidental. A single model, Frank Dolson, was used for all the men and even for one of the women in the tree. "He's got a good face," Norman Rockwell wrote in his chronicle of the painting, "strong jaw, mouth, nose (the broad bridge is a characteristic which will carry through from a pirate to the modern man very nicely—noticeable but not obtrusive, so that the pirate's descendants will bear a family resemblance to each other, but won't look exactly alike); heavy eyebrows."

Posing for Rockwell, Frank Dolson changed his facial expression to suit the various roles, a matter of purely subjective interpretation: "Look like a pirate. Now look like a rancher. Now look like a preacher's wife," Rockwell commanded as Clem Kalischer recorded the subtle differences with his camera. Any Rockwells in the tree?, one might ask. Exactly two: daughter-in-law Gail (Tom Rockwell's wife) is the southern belle, and the illustrator elected himself to portray the preacher. 🐛

Family Tree. Original oil painting for a *Saturday Evening Post* cover, October 24, 1959. Old Corner House Collection, Stockbridge, Massachusetts.

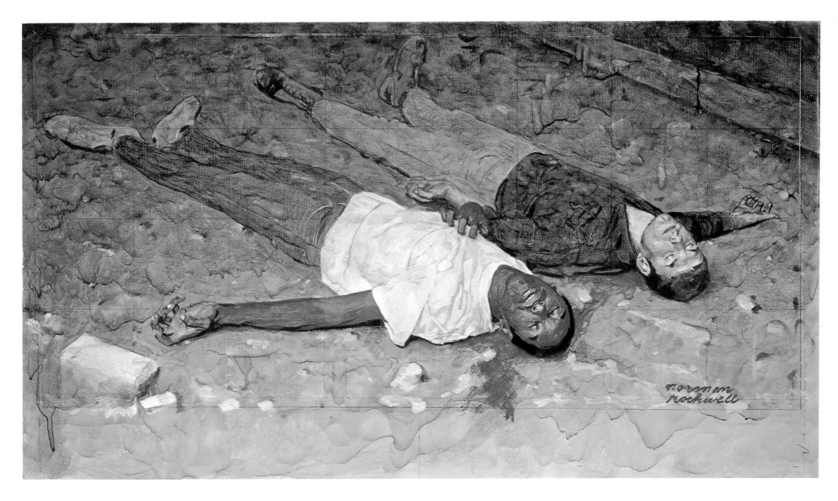

ABOVE AND OPPOSITE: *Civil Rights Sketches.* Originals for *Look* magazine, June 29, 1965. Old Corner House Collection, Stockbridge, Massachusetts.

Norman Rockwell's work took a decidedly more political turn during the 1960s, a far cry from his reluctance to put a black face at the bottom of the *Family Tree* only a few years before. His shift had less to do with his personal politics—he had always been a liberal—than it did with the fact that he began to express his political ideas in his illustrations. Several factors influenced this development. The 1960s witnessed events that produced major upheavals—the civil rights movement, the Cuba missile crisis, John F. Kennedy's

assassination—generating widespread public reaction. And the magazines reaching this public responded in kind. With the demise of the *Post*, Rockwell found himself engaged with other publications that encouraged him to depict controversial subjects. *Look* magazine, in particular, published several of these subjects by Rockwell. The illustrator's eagerness to give vent to his convictions was supported—indeed encouraged—by his new wife, Molly. These illustrations brought Rockwell into a new arena, and he thrived on it.

OVERLEAF: *The Problem We All Live With.* Original oil painting for *Look* magazine, January 14, 1964. Old Corner House Collection, Stockbridge, Massachusetts.

The seventy-year-old Norman Rockwell, renowned for his innocent domestic scenes, managed once again to astonish his audience. The sheer bravura of this composition is evidence of his mastery: painting on an enormous canvas, Rockwell cropped four of the five bodies in order to focus on the smallest figure in the painting, an artistic choice that would be disastrous in the hands of a less capable artist. The apparent simplicity of the composition is also deceptive. The gaping space

between the girl and the men marching behind her—a space that represents about two-fifths of the entire canvas—would have been deadly were it not for Rockwell's skillful treatment of the tomato-stained concrete wall. Rockwell may have been an elderly artist when he undertook this scene in the tranquillity of his Stockbridge studio, but he was still taking the kind of risks even painters far younger would never attempt.

rockwell

Norman Rockwell

PORTRAIT OF THE ARTIST

Norman Rockwell appears in many of his own paintings. As a secondary figure, he frequently made an Alfred Hitchcock-like cameo appearance, eyes twinkling out from a lower corner of a painting, a profile in a crowd, an incidental head in a family tree. Designed for his own entertainment, these casual appearances were unexpected details that exemplified Rockwell's wry humor. So basic to his illustration, his humor was equally characteristic in his demeanor: a tendency to play the joke on himself, at his own expense, free of cruelty or sarcasm. "He took his work seriously," said Don Spaulding, "but he didn't take himself seriously."

Rockwell's talent for poking fun at himself was acquired during boyhood, when he was an awkward, knock-kneed adolescent who wore corrective shoes and round spectacles that earned him the name Moonface or Mooney. Turning the laughter inward reduced the sting of humiliation; his light-hearted antics became known by his family as "Norman's stunts." Laughter was, for Rockwell, a means of conveying sympathy for the poignant experiences shared by even the most arrogant of souls, a gentle reminder that we're all human.

Still more revealing were his self-portraits in which he portrayed himself at the easel, his back to the viewer, a man whose essence was realized through images privately conceived and rendered. Yet through this essentially solitary process, Norman Rockwell reached millions of Americans, an audience that perceived in these images a simple truth expressed without pretense. From his adolescent days when he felt like "a lump, a long skinny nothing," until he worked at the easel from a wheelchair, Norman Rockwell satisfied his deepest needs and yearnings through his art. His work brought him love, and being loved counted most of all.

Rockwell's work and character were consistent. The humor and gentleness, the sentiment and modesty so evident in his paintings were the very qualities he presented to those he encountered every day. "If something went wrong," said Louie Lamone, "he always blamed himself, not the other guy. Once I made a terrible mistake about something and all Norman said was, 'I guess you're human after all,' not angry with me for having fouled up with his business." Walter Scott observed a similar quality in Rockwell: "Norman was incapable of complaining about anything." "I never saw him

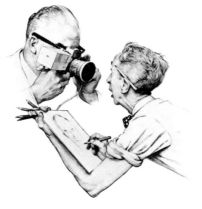

The portrait of the artist as seen through the lens of a camera was a subject that appealed to Rockwell. Here Barry Goldwater photographs the artist as the artist depicts Barry Goldwater.

angry," said Buddy Edgerton. He was thoughtful about small details and his friends never forgot it. On his trips abroad Rockwell always remembered to bring back something to his friends. If Louie Lamone happened to arrive in the studio early in the morning, Rockwell often thought to bring him a cup of coffee, "even before he had his own breakfast. He didn't care who you were. He would never talk down or make me feel as if I weren't his equal." "He was the kindest man I ever knew," said Chris Schafer.

Detail from *Soldier's Homecoming.*

Throughout his life, Norman Rockwell played to his audience like an actor. Keenly sensitive to his public, Rockwell depicted attitudes that might not conform to his own views but would touch his public. His opinions could be quite separate—though not in contradiction—from those expressed in his paintings. Rockwell's mission, as he saw it, was to be in harmony with his public, not to challenge popular convictions. He was not a moralist, and he didn't pretend to be: "I have always wanted everybody to like my work. I could never be satisfied with just the approval of the critics (and, boy, I've certainly had to be satisfied without it) or a small group of kindred souls. So I have painted pictures that didn't disturb anybody, that I knew everyone would understand and like. (Everybody who comes into my studio from the grocery boy to the vice president of an advertising agency has to comment on the picture I'm painting and I take all comments to heart.)"

Detail from *Poor Richard's Almanack.*

Only in later years, partly in response to pressures from his family and partly because the post-War audience would accept it, did he portray more controversial issues in his paintings. Rockwell was more progressive in his politics that his public might have assumed. He wanted to paint a black Boy Scout, for example, long before such subjects were acceptable to the general public. Likewise, his sense of fairness enabled him to paint portraits of all the presidential candidates in a given election, regardless of his own preferences.

This is not to say that Rockwell was inauthentic in his work. "He believed in what he painted. That's why his work is so good," said Mead Schaeffer. No imitator of Rockwell—and there have been many—has been successful in duplicating Rockwell, simply because an artist's work is more than a visual phenomenon; it is a manifestation of the inner person. Rockwell was genuine. Over the years he developed an outlook that enabled him to cope with pain. An unfortunate situation could be rendered tolerable—even pleasant—with a slight twist of reality. Said Rockwell, "Maybe as I grew up and found that the world wasn't the perfectly pleasant place I had thought it to be, I unconsciously decided that, even if it wasn't an ideal world, it should be so and so I painted only the ideal aspects of it. . . . If there was sadness in this created world of mine, it was a pleasant sadness. If there were problems, they were humorous problems."

Detail from *The Gossips.*

Rockwell was amply rewarded for his optimism. The adulation he received from his public through his paintings and his loving personal relations

Detail from *The Forging Contest.*

Detail from *Family Homecoming*.

Detail from *Family Tree*.

Detail from *Golden Rule*.

Detail from *University Club*.

reinforced what he painted and how he performed. He exposed few people to his deep inner conflicts. He always managed a cheerful greeting for a neighbor. Even while Mary Rockwell was ill and he was undergoing psychiatric treatment himself—shattered by the sadness he felt for his wife and discouraged about the direction of his own work—he conveyed enthusiasm and high spirits to his models, to his neighbors, and to his friends. In his painting and in his personal relations he protected others (and himself, one suspects) from the harsh realities of a world that "wasn't the perfectly pleasant place" it should be. He must have paid a substantial personal price for this kindly deception.

Because he played to his public—and was a superb actor—he tended to exaggerate some of the qualities he felt his public wanted to see in him. His Will Rogers manner was not a false persona, by any means, but he was a good deal more cosmopolitan than his public demeanor suggested. "Norman was no hayseed," said George Hughes. Peter Rockwell agreed. "In public he was conscious that he was a famous person and to some extent he performed accordingly. He was actually a serious and intelligent thinker, but played that down because he felt his audience wanted him to be more folksy."

He *was* conscious of his fame and he thrived on it. Even on this subject, however, he did not overlook the joke on himself. Characteristically, he made fun of his susceptibility to vanity. Peter Rockwell recalled his father's return from a second trip to Moscow. The illustrator confessed that the trip had been a bit trying because no one in the city seemed to recognize him. Walking down a street in Moscow on the third day of their visit, Molly and Norman Rockwell saw a familiar flash of recognition come over the face of a gentleman approaching them. Prepared for the gratifying greeting ahead, Rockwell extended his hand enthusiastically. The man was thrilled, indeed: "Why, you must be Molly Punderson's husband," he exclaimed, looking into Norman Rockwell's disappointed eyes. So much for international fame.

Rockwell was more flattered when he was talking with Russians and was informed that an entire floor at the Hermitage had been devoted to a permanent display of his paintings. Later he discovered they had confused his name with that of Rockwell Kent, the American painter who was persona non grata in the United States because he had made no secret of his admiration for the Soviets at a time when such affection was most unpopular in America. But Norman Rockwell? Never heard of him.

In America such moments of anonymity were rare, of course. In later years, when his face was as familiar as the *Saturday Evening Post* itself, Rockwell was pursued by fans who pleaded for a handshake, an autograph, a memento to take home to the family. Rockwell was an obliging celebrity. He shook hands and autographed every piece of paper held before him, always with a smile and a personal acknowledgment. During the day a neighbor could feel free to leave a book on the kitchen table for him to sign. The next day the neigbor would return and the signed book would be waiting where it had been left. When Rockwell was very advanced in years, no longer able to paint, he signed dozens of prints every evening. He enjoyed doing it.

Jarvis Rockwell remembered being with his aged father one day when the sound of children's voices outside brought Rockwell out of the doldrums. "He came to life when he saw the kids. He joked with them, signed autographs, and told a story. After they left, Pop withdrew again into his dark mood, like an animal in a cave. The children made him feel like his old self for a moment. He loved his public."

Within Rockwell's character mingled an odd mixture of supreme self-confidence with fretful feelings of inadequacy. His self-assurance enabled him to attack the most ambitious painting problems—such as *Shuffleton's Barbershop* and *Saying Grace*, two very complex compositions—setting standards of excellence that demanded he summon all his artistic resources. As a student, Don Spaulding was astonished at Rockwell's daring at the easel.

Rockwell was not embarrassed to take credit for his achievements either. His signature—where it was placed and how it was indicated—was important to him, one of the first decisions he made. Walter Scott remembers Rockwell's blank canvas. Before any of the painting was laid in, the canvas was set in a frame and the signature already indicated. Rockwell felt the signature should be clear and obvious to the viewer, because he considered the artist's name an important aspect of an illustration. He placed his name carefully—in block letters, cursive writing, or initials—to suit the composition, easily located, but not intrusive.

"Rockwell presented his work in the best possible way. You had to take it seriously," observed Don Spaulding, "by the size he painted his pictures and by the way he framed them. So many artists shipped their paintings down to the *Post* tacked to a shabby mat board. Norman was never so casual. All his pictures were delivered by hand. As large as they were, they came framed beautifully, like important paintings from The Metropolitan Museum of Art."

This attention to the signature and to the presentation suggests a man who felt his work was worthy. By contrast he could be indecisive. He asked advice over and over. ("Pop always needed everyone's opinion on every subject that mattered to him," said Jarvis Rockwell.) Getting many opinions on a subject of personal or professional importance was his method of thinking through a problem. To consider all points of view was a painstaking process that inevitably led to a decision. But he never relaxed. Rockwell was fully aware that to remain at the top he had to perform over and over again. In spite of repeated successes, he never altogether lost his fear of falling out of favor. When he thought the *Post* was going out of business in 1942, he felt a mixture of sorrow and relief. "By 1942 I had been painting

Beyond the Easel. Original oil painting. ©1969 Brown & Bigelow, Inc., a Division of Saxon Industries, Inc. Collection Boy Scouts of America.

Post covers for twenty-six years. It had been a constant challenge. If a cover was unpopular, I felt my work was sagging and, becoming scared, thought, I'll be dropped from the *Post*. Every new illustrator had been a threat. Perhaps he'll be better than I, I'd thought, and force me off the *Post*. So for twenty-six years I'd had to prove myself all over again with each cover I did." The *Post* did not fold in 1942, and Rockwell continued to work with the same apprehension as he had for the previous twenty-six years.

No doubt Rockwell's work managed to stay fresh for nearly six decades *because* he continually re-evaluated his efforts. "I know I'm not satisfied with my work," he said. "At times it seems shallow, incomplete. But that keeps me working. If I thought I was perfect or even close to it, I'd probably pawn my brushes and quit." He worried that he was stagnating, that he was losing his freshness, and he continually sought methods of re-energizing his approach. "Now and again the pressure builds up and I begin to worry about being old fashioned, outside the mainstream of art in our age," Rockwell recalled. "Most times I rid myself of this feeling by experimenting with new techniques. But every so often I try a whole new approach." In the early 1930s he experimented with Dynamic Symmetry, then fashionable, and went to study in Paris. Mary Rockwell's letters written from Paris (see Appendix) verify the depth of his artistic struggle during this period in Rockwell's life. Jarvis Rockwell remembered his father, much later in his career, studying two reproductions placed at the foot of his bed—one by the fifteenth-century painter Piero della Francesca and the other by the Abstract Expressionist Willem de Kooning. Rockwell admired the former but struggled with the thought that he might have missed some important lesson in the modern painter.

This fear of falling behind might lead him to attack a subject more familiar to his younger colleagues at the *Post*—Stevan Dohanos, John Falter, or George Hughes—a contemporary theme, such as television or suburban living, perhaps. The results were unconvincing. ("A disaster," Rockwell said about his new approaches. "I have enough sense to know I can't do anything but my own kind of work.")

The single artistic pursuit that haunted him for years was "the big picture," a pictorial statement of universal importance. He came close to achieving this goal with two of his *Four Freedoms*. (Rockwell was relatively satisfied with *Freedom of Worship* and *Freedom of Speech*, whereas "neither of the other two," he said, "has any wallop.") The hope of painting "the big picture" never altogether left him, and he felt compelled to try it over and over. None of his attempts was totally effective. He started—and never finished—a painting on the United Nations; he followed with *The Golden Rule* as a *Post* cover and *The Right To Know* as an illustration for *Look*. His paintings of the Peace Corps, the War on Poverty, and the team of Apollo 11 were additional attempts. "By dropping his story telling, he dropped one of his best elements," Peter Rockwell explained. Rockwell was a vulnerable man, given to sentiment and easily moved by simple gestures of feeling. Surrendering to this tendency meant creating paintings that were too sentimental, a danger he fought in every painting. At its best, this quality produced some of his finest work. Paintings such as *Saying Grace* and *Breaking Home Ties* succeeded so well because they were honest responses to deeply felt experiences. If he failed with others, he did so because he became too sentimental.

Above all, it was Rockwell's profound humanism that distinguished him. He was to his art what his favorite writers were to their novels: Dickens, Tolstoy, Mark Twain, and Thackeray. Like them, Rockwell delighted in the idiosyncrasy, individuality, and eccentricity of those he observed around him. Like them, he placed his individuals within a universal context, casting his characters in an extraordinary pageant of familiar life experiences. This vast parade of personalities and situations made life worth living for him. He observed the human condition and celebrated it with a loving brush. In the end, by sharing his affection for humanity, Norman Rockwell gave as much love to his people as he received.

This is as serious a self-portrait as Pop could do," observed Peter Rockwell. As an appraisal of the portrait, this statement expresses much about the artist himself. The *Triple Self-Portrait* is a summation of Rockwell as an artist. This is not simply a collection of familiar furniture surrounding him. The details here represent the artist's history, they document his personal and professional tastes: a glass of Coke, a dog-eared art book, a metal trash bucket that protects a smoldering match from spreading into flame, the signature on a nearly blank canvas, and the spectrum of painters who inspired him throughout his life—Albrecht Dürer, Rembrandt, Pablo Picasso, Vincent Van Gogh. Typically, each of these details has a descriptive purpose, as well as a function in the design structure of the painting. Not one detail has been carelessly selected or placed in the composition. Given his precision—his aversion to ambivalent meaning in his narrative work—it is impossible to overlook the suggestive handling of the face itself. Why are his eyes totally concealed by the eyeglasses in the reflection and featured so prominently on the canvas? Was he suggesting that he was one man in the mirror and another in his art? Rockwell left open the possibility that he was simply playing games in the painting, a characteristic trait, but this self-portrayal might also have been his psychological interpretation of the man *behind* the easel as well. ❧

Triple Self-Portrait. Original oil painting for a *Saturday Evening Post* cover, February 13, 1960. Old Corner House Collection, Stockbridge, Massachusetts.

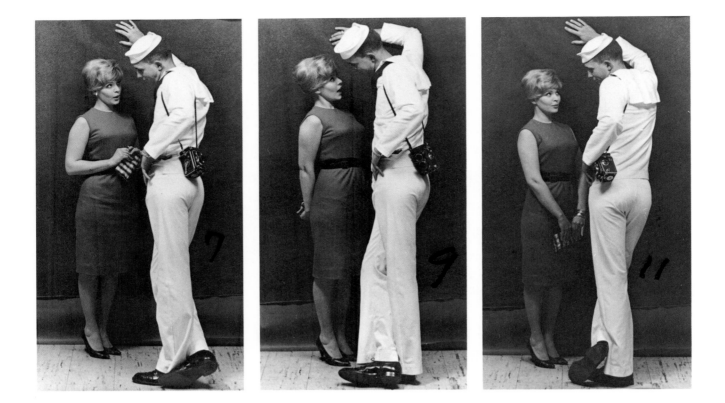

In later years Rockwell tended to go farther afield for his subjects. He traveled more and was less intimately connected to the specific people in his pictures. He brought his photographer to the University Club in New York City for this cover and painted his models from a distant view. Peter Rockwell remembers how much fun his father had painting the sailor, and Rockwell himself remarked, "The peculiar way a sailor stands when talking to a girl—slouched above her, left leg straight, hip out, right leg bent at knee, right arm propped on wall behind her head—has always fascinated me." The girl receiving all the attention was a movie starlet at the time, a young actress named Gen Melia. Just for fun, of course, Rockwell inserted himself in the lower left corner and added Gail, his son Tom's wife, as well.

University Club. Original oil painting for a *Saturday Evening Post* cover, August 27, 1960.

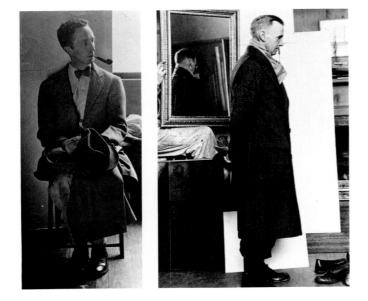

During the war, the nearest ration board to Arlington was in Manchester, Vermont, which explains why Rockwell selected most of his models for the painting from that town. (Only Jessie Harrington, the man standing at the table, was living in Arlington at the time.) It was like Rockwell to place himself in a painting to demonstrate his feeling of membership in a community. He included himself in *The Gossips* in order not to offend his neighbors. After all, he was no different from them. Here he is simply the next in line, waiting to see his local ration board during the war. He did not perceive himself as special or exceptional. Even achieving the status of a celebrity did not spoil him. His sense of humanity derived from his authentic connection to those around him. To alter that bond would have destroyed the lifeblood of the artist. 🐛

NORMAN ROCKWELL VISITS A Ration Board

SPRING was on the land, and the benignant Vermont sun, having penetrated every other nook and cranny in the town of Manchester, presently made its way into a certain quiet room where six men and one woman sat around a long, plain table. Then, in the following order, came: The song of birds, the fragrance of flowers, and—Norman Rockwell.

The last of these three, it developed, wanted something. The ration board, never having had a visitor who didn't, evinced no surprise. In Rockwell's case, however, the desideratum was none of the things that the rest of us try to wheedle out of our ration boards.

"What I would like," said America's favorite artist, "is the privilege of painting pictures of all you board members."

Could it have been a glow of pleasure, the stirring of some long-suppressed vanity, that seemed momentarily to illumine the seven faces? After all, New Englanders are human. And when Rockwell paints you, the world sees you. At any rate, the board members consulted one another, reached a decision, and in unison nodded to the artist.

"But make us look good, now."

In a flash, Rockwell saw his advantage. Living in New England sharpens a man, brings out the trader in him.

"If I do," he bargained, "will you give me a B card?"

Seven pairs of eyes converged upon the confident, half-smiling visitor. Living in New England helps, of course, but it doesn't put a man in the same class with people who were born there.

"No, but if you don't," they said, "we'll take away your A card."

In a flash, Rockwell took a back seat (the same one you see him occupying a few inches to the right of where your eyes are now) and, his favorite pipe in his mouth, spent all day—a day of sunshine and showers—watching America parade by.

It was a parade that has been and still is going on all over the Union; a parade which differs from all other parades in this—everybody marches in it. That is why it interested Rockwell. It is an integral part of the American scene—now. There was no such thing a few years ago, and who can say how soon our ration boards will disband and this unique parade vanish forever? But no matter; for Rockwell has recorded the scene—the ration board at work and (below) the importunate citizens who appear before it.

That record, reproduced here, is the newest chapter of a book which has been in the making for twenty-eight consecutive years. The book might well be entitled Norman Rockwell's History of the U.S.A. It contains no text, and needs none. To leaf through its pages is to know America as it was—how its people looked and acted, how they dreamed and mourned and grinned—between the years 1915 and 1944.

Other chapters will be added from time to time. Many of them, we trust. In fact, we would like to see them just keep on appearing indefinitely—and in the Post.

—The Editors.

Norman Rockwell Visits a Ration Board. Original oil painting for a *Saturday Evening Post* series, July 15, 1944.

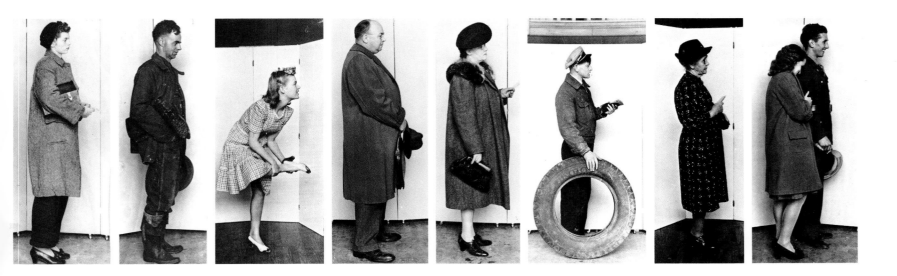

Oil sketch for *Norman Rockwell Visits a Country Editor*. Old Corner House Collection, Stockbridge, Massachusetts.

Rockwell's membership in the publishing community no doubt inspired him to include himself in the offices of the country editor. The newspaper office was actually located in the midwest, but the atmosphere of the place was probably no different from that in any other town, and Rockwell's presence hardly seems to matter. He was unlikely to impose himself on a new situation anyway, and would certainly not have stolen the thunder from his own illustration. 🍎

Visit to a Country Editor. Original oil painting for a *Saturday Evening Post* series, May 25, 1946.

OVERLEAF:

While he was painting other luminaries of the 1960s for *Saturday People*—Ringo Starr, Jonathan Winters, Prince Philip, Leonard Bernstein—Norman Rockwell included his wife and himself in the group. He was not unaware of his fame—on the contrary, he flourished in it—but he had not lost his modesty either. In the end what nourished him, what integrated the extremes between his private and public selves, was his work. Without it, life was over. ❦

Saturday People. Original oil painting for illustration, *McCall's* magazine, October, 1966. Old Corner House Collection, Stockbridge, Massachusetts.

Sketch for *Golden Rule*.

"The big picture": that's what Norman Rockwell wanted to paint for years, a universal statement about humanity. Perhaps the idea was greater than any artist had a right to entertain, but he felt he had come so close with *The Four Freedoms* and was compelled to try again. *The Golden Rule* did not succeed. Nor, for that matter, did any other Rockwell painting come close to fulfilling the artist's ambition. But *The Golden Rule* is a marvelous painting in other ways: it is a panorama of Rockwell's people, a gathering of the friends and relatives he had loved through the years.

The big picture was originally started in Arlington many years before as a tribute to the United Nations. It was an enormous undertaking. Rockwell spent five months producing fifty portraits for a ten-foot-long charcoal, then photographing and reassembling them into a composition of twenty-eight heads for the finished painting. In addition to these assorted subjects, Rockwell intended to include the delegates to the Security Council at the United Nations, the chief representatives from the United States, United Kingdom, Soviet Union, and Chile. The first two subjects were acceptable, if somewhat forbidding, but Rockwell encountered insufferable frustrations in getting the Soviet Union delegate, Andrei Vishinsky,

to pose. When Vishinsky was finally replaced with another delegate, leaving Rockwell to start all over, the artist threw up his hands and abandoned the project altogether.

Rockwell recovered the charcoal drawing of the United Nations tribute when he prepared his cover for the 1961 *Post* cover. From his file he pulled out the old photographs he had taken of his Arlington neighbors—Rose Hoyt and her child, Jim McCabe, Gene Pelham, Buddy Edgerton—and integrated these with subjects from the Stockbridge area—a Japanese student from Bennington College, a Brazilian boy, a Chinese girl living in Pittsfield, an Arab from Stockbridge, a retired postmaster. During his recent travels around the world, Rockwell had acquired costumes which he used to good advantage in the painting. The faces and costumes changed as he developed the painting. Some were added, others taken away. The group in *The Golden Rule* evolved into a gathering of distant and intimate friends. In the upper right-hand corner, immediately behind Chris Schafer, Rockwell painted his wife Mary, who had died only recently. In Mary Rockwell's arms is the grandchild— her first—whom she never knew. Geoffrey Rockwell was born less than four months after she passed away. 🍎

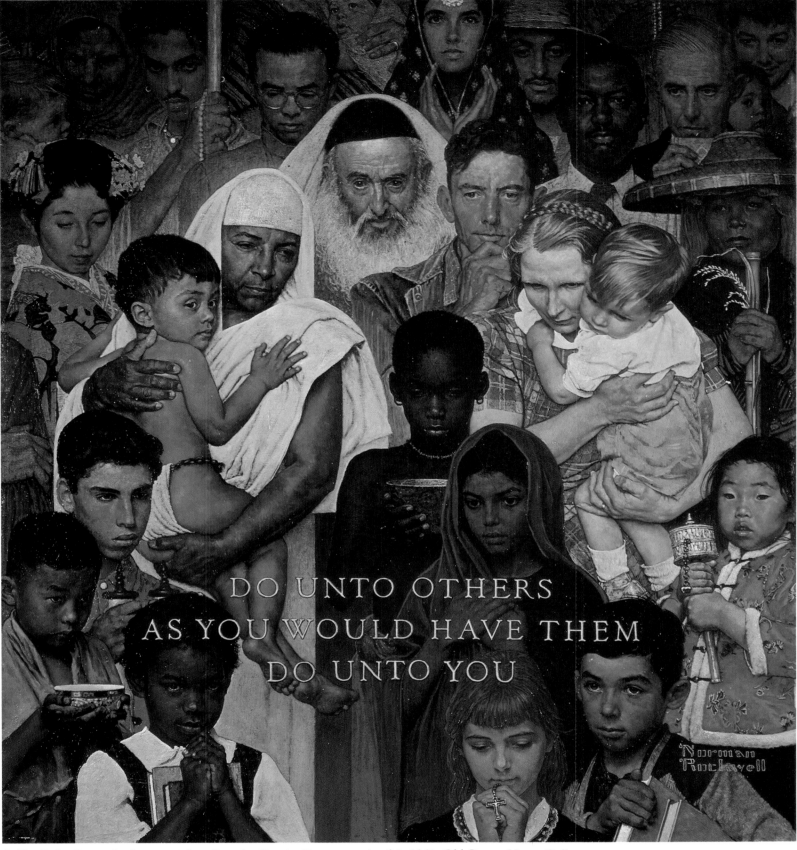

DO UNTO OTHERS
AS YOU WOULD HAVE THEM
DO UNTO YOU

Golden Rule. Original oil painting for a *Saturday Evening Post* cover, April 1, 1961. Old Corner House Collection, Stockbridge, Massachusetts.

March 8:

We rode down to the boat very peacefully in a large [Pierce Arrow taxi] with our numerous bags and Jerry [six months old] and Raleigh [the Rockwell's German shepherd] whom there was scarcely room for—not so peaceful.

Can't you see us—me leading the dog—Norm carrying Jerry—followed by the luggage ascending the fortunately vacant gang plank.

Norm at last has a studio which is perfect. It is in an old studio building on the Avenue de Saxe. . . . It has a direct north light, grey walls and a coal stove and—piece de resistance—a couch and shelves in a corner all covered with deep wine colored velvet. It's really nice and the woman had an easel Norm could use. He bought a table, a stool, put out his sketches and a clothes tree with costumes until it looks very homelike and exactly the place to work.

April 11, 1932:

And now the best thing of all that I have to tell you is about Norman's work. The preliminary struggle, nearly two years long, has ended at last and he knows what he wants to do. He sent a final cable to Snyder and Black, refusing to do the Cocoa Cola, but letting them use his name. (He couldn't do less as he had see-sawed between yes and no so long.) He has indefinitely postponed his Post covers. I personally rather doubt if he'll do any more.

You see this was all decided once in America, but was much harder to adhere to there. He got scared at the idea of so complete a change, worked furiously and got up four good Post ideas, and with those as security, sailed. I was sure he wouldn't want to do them, but fortunately I kept still. It's funny, I can often prophesy what will happen to him way ahead of time. When we got here he worked until a week ago on the picture he started at home, the story book characters marching along—only changing it and

putting them in an enchanted forest which is much better. He never worked so hard before, but he really loved it and wanted to work on it, so he was never discouraged. But a week ago knowing C. C. had to be in by May 15th and insisting he must do a Post cover first—he started one. Well, he worked four days and tried a brand new La Got-taist technique in a different kind of paint, used at least six canvases, got thoroughly mixed up, discouraged, upset, cold in the chest (better now) and so on. The reason he tried [a] new technique was because he couldn't bear to do the same old thing and doing a Post cover meant that unless you changed completely. He kept worrying because he didn't really like most modern things and so wasn't going with the trend. Then he got a new model and took a day off before starting. He went to a modern gallery and then the Louvre and got so excited he rushed back to get . . . me, and we went to the modern exhibit and then spent the rest of the afternoon at the Louvre (which is the most thrilling place I think I've ever been). He and I spent two hours there before I went off to luncheon and when we came out the die was cast. I told the model and he called Snyder and Black. Today he is doing the last preliminary work before painting on the big picture and tomorrow he is going to begin the first of three days sketching around Paris. For the first time in his life he is going to be a free man and do every thing he really wants to do.

April 25th:

Truly, this trip is the best thing that ever happened to us. It has made Norman a different person. He has found the courage to do what he wants for six months which shows that after two years of struggling—and it truly was that—he has at last come out in the open and knows what he wants to do, which is experiment with all sorts of things for the next six months so become an artistic artist instead of a commercial one. Don't fear that he will go modern. That is his last thought. Never. For a while that worried him; but as I told you the Louvre inspires him and modern galleries do not, so now he's decided to be the thing that is in him to be—to do what he did, only in a much finer way.

You see for two years before we were married, while he was going with that crowd, he was drawing on all his past reserve. After the divorce and our marriage he was a different person entirely, but his work went on being the same and all during the first two years we were married he was trying, blindly at first, to reconcile the two. Finally we got desperate—the pressure of people and things in New Rochelle was too much, though we saw them seldom; it all weighed on us terribly so somehow or other we found the courage to come over here which was the best thing we ever could have done.

You should see us start off sketching in the morning; Norman in a hat with turned down brim, a pipe, a raincoat, sketching outfit slung over one shoulder and a stool in his other hand; me with a suit and the polo coat, a beret, and flat heeled shoes, which no Frenchman fails to gaze at—and how they stare here! and a well stuffed bag under my arm . . .

May 9th:

But the important thing is about Norman's work. I last told you about how he had decided to experiment. That didn't satisfy him for long so he and I thought and talked a great deal more, went to the Louvre and he decided that the only thing he really wanted to do was the same sort of thing he'd always done so we felt much better. He got models, made a charming charcoal layout and then something stopped him, he couldn't figure out what. Finally he realized that in taking an old Post cover subject he'd gone to the other extreme which really wasn't himself any more; so after a good deal of agony he suddenly realized that the thing he wanted to do was a picture that he had planned to do before he came over but had gotten side tracked on. So he found his models and started today. I'm sure all will go right now.

We have made a big decision; to move out of New Rochelle the minute we can find a place somewhere in Connecticut with some ground and a Colonial house. We couldn't stand going back to New Rochelle!

about May 20th:

Three days ago Norman moved his studio to a small studio apartment . . . altogether more comfortable and prac-

ticable. There is also a kitchen and a bedroom where he can store things and where his models can dress, and, the prize feature, a toilet. In the other studio he had to go down three flights to find one, which is not convenient. The other apartment on the floor is rented by a young art student, Alan Haemer . . . So that is awfully nice for Norman, because there is some one near him, a man, and an artist with whom to talk things over. Today he started his illustrator picture for the fourth time, and I'm quite sure the final time as everything seems to be straightened out now.

June 10th:

Now, please do not be worried about Norman. . . . he is just going through a period of transition which is necessary to an honest artist when he is changing the purpose or direction of his work. Before he had few thoughts beyond Post covers. Now he wants to do much finer things, but of the same human sort, and probably he will do some covers again when he gets straightened out. . . . He says he feels for the first time as if he knew what he was doing.

. . . I, though I had two strong opinions about the picture when I entered the room, mentioned neither of them but let Norman come around to them himself. You see he is so honest that he will always see things for himself, if you give him time and it is much better to do that than to force your opinion upon him. Having tried the right way once, I know I will have no trouble again. . . . What I can do, however, is to ask leading questions, and clarify the atmosphere when he gets too involved, by bringing him back to the question, and explaining when he asks advice that he is the only one who can decide the question, and he has to do it by searching inside himself for the thing he instinctively feels. So I think I have discovered a good working combination.

June 19th:

I have one big tremendous announcement to make—no, not another child—but its equivalent—a picture finished. I've written you of Norman's struggles. You see he came over here to learn to paint in the way that was natural to him now, not to repeat the old thing that was no longer part of him—did not express his present self. So each time he felt a picture was doing that, something instinctively honest in him made him stop doing it. This happened so many times that, as you can imagine he got pretty desperate in a way. So finally just a week ago he decided to do the illustrations for a story the Journal wanted him to do. Well, it was like a miracle, all at once he got hold of a technique, far easier and far more artistic (I mean genuinely so, good composition, simplicity, pattern) and yet retaining every bit of the character and charm that his people have always had, but with infinitely more real spirit and freedom about. He worked terribly hard on it, but it doesn't look worked at all. . . . now he feels he has something he can develop and go on and on with instead of working right up against a flat wall all the time as he has since we have been married. So it has all been worth while, all the agony and struggle he has been through. It's funny and nice; through it all he's always had more work than he could possibly do—[the] Depression not withstanding. . . .

To continue, the Post keeps telegraphing N. to ask how he is and how his work is going, which is flattering.

July 29th:

As I said, we shall probably go home in October as Norm feels he should see his mother and my longing for familiar things and sudden eschewal of drink and cigarettes would point to the fact that another member of the family is on the way, which I am very glad about as I am very fit . . . and especially because Norm is *so* tickled. . . .

I have other even better news. The day I have been waiting for for two years arrived yesterday and Norm came home with the definite knowledge and feeling that his problem is completely solved and that whole new worlds are opened to him. The Journal illustrations were the first step. And characteristically enough he found the solution on a Post cover. You know how grand his charcoal layouts have always been, and how more and more he has hated to spend two weeks finishing up in oil. Well, yesterday he finished more than one figure in less than a day (he used to take at least four). With the solid background of his layout he washed on color and does all sorts of things, difficult to explain but with a result that is a thousand times more artistic and spirited and thrilling than anything he ever did. . . . It will take him perhaps five days at most to do a Post cover now whereas before it took two weeks time. . . . And now he feels he can do so many things that with his old technique he couldn't touch.

August 9th:

Norm is simply getting along marvelously now. He just sent off two Post covers. And now, having found a different technique in which he feels there are possibilities, he feels free to experiment to his hearts content, which means he is really going to be an artist. . . . it is going to be perfect if the Post approves of his new covers. . . .

Between Aug. 10th and 18th:

Of course our present decision [to remain in Paris] rests on what we hear from the Post concerning the two covers he just sent over. I have no doubt what we'll hear. Of course he has. But when we do hear favorably it means that he can spend five days a week making income each month and the rest of the time painting.

Aug. 18th:

The other day we decided to go back and live in New York this winter. The difficulty is that we are still awaiting word from the Post about the two covers, which makes Norman just as upset as possible, though he is bearing up nobly and working on the Boy Scout calendar.

INDEX

Numbers in roman type refer to text pages.
Numbers in *italic* type refer to pages on
which illustrations appear.